KEEGAN

by the same author

KLOPP: MY LIVERPOOL ROMANCE

KEEGAN

The Man Who Was King

ANTHONY QUINN

faber

First published in 2025
by Faber & Faber Limited
The Bindery, 51 Hatton Garden
London EC1N 8HN
First published in the USA in 2025

Typeset by Ian Bahrami
Printed and bound in the UK by CPI Group (UK) Ltd,
Croydon CR0 4YY

A CIP record for this book
is available from the British Library

ISBN 978–0–571–39225–4

MIX
Paper | Supporting
responsible forestry
FSC® C013604

Printed and bound in the UK on FSC® certified paper in line with our continuing
commitment to ethical business practices, sustainability and the environment.
For further information see faber.co.uk/environmental-policy

Our authorised representative in the EU for product safety is
Easy Access System Europe, Mustamäe tee 50, 10621 Tallinn, Estonia
gpsr.requests@easproject.com

2 4 6 8 10 9 7 5 3 1

For Stephen Browett

Ah, but a man's reach should exceed his grasp,
Or what's a heaven for?

Robert Browning

CONTENTS

INTRODUCTION

They used to call him Joe. There he is, in a two-minute black-and-white clip on YouTube, a short, raw-boned kid buzzing around the training ground with that busy, scuttling run, the day so cold his breath plumes. It's actually a rugby pitch (you can see the posts) but needs must for Scunthorpe United of the Fourth Division. Now the kid is talking in his soft Yorkshire accent to Gerald Sinstadt, Granada TV's voice of football in the North. Up close you can see how shy he is, unable to catch the interviewer's eye, or the camera's, and yet touchingly polite. Sinstadt says that people are talking about him as a player of the future – is he conscious of that? 'I ain't heard owt,' he replies. 'I'm conscious of it, p'raps, but I try not to be. Or I try not to let people see I am.' The ghost of a smile. Would he welcome the chance to move to another club? 'Depends what sort of club, really. I'm 'appy here . . . should think if I went First Division, I'd struggle a bit.'

In fact, he was bound for the First Division the next year, and it wouldn't be a struggle for him at all. Television had just had its first glimpse of Joseph Kevin Keegan.

As a player, Keegan would bestride the game like a fun-size colossus. As a manager, he would come close to greatness, before an epic stumble unseated him. What happened? Did his ambition overreach his talent, or was he by temperament an individualist who couldn't work with a group? Perhaps the answer is something larger to do with sport and the people who watch it. When we think about Kevin Keegan we picture a young player, a Tigger in his red Liverpool FC top and jet helmet of hair, scoring a goal at the Kop end, raising his arms to the fans. We also think of him as the aggrieved, haggard-faced manager wearing huge headphones and ranting before the Sky TV camera as it all gets too much. *I will love it if we beat them, love it . . .*

Two faces of Kev, and two facets of football: the winner and the loser.

Only it's not as simple as that. The game, for those of us who watch it, is about enjoyment. It's about the pleasure of watching players compete, be brave, score goals. It's also about luck. If we only watched it for the result, it would be a dull old world. If fans cared only about winning, why would they bother following a football club? We know how few teams will ever come close to winning a trophy. That's the philosophical hazard of being a fan. It's about endurance as well as enjoyment; the tribal aspect of being with your mates; the ritual aspect of singing and chanting and eating a bad pie; the theatrical aspect of watching talent perform. A 90-minute enthralment that offers a holiday from the real world. Winning is merely a bonus. If you lose? Well, don't knock the pleasure of moaning, of commiserating, of laughing at your own misfortune. Losing is so deeply intrinsic to football it's almost encoded in the word itself. Your team lost – but does that make them 'losers'? No. It just makes *you* disappointed.

Disappointment is something hard-wired into everyone who plays or watches sport. It's the default condition of supporting a club. Disappointment is not the same thing as failure, though they're related. You can win at something and still feel disappointed. Witness the Keegan rant: you wouldn't know it, but his Newcastle team had won that day (they had beaten Leeds 1–0). I used to live in a flat about five hundred yards from a big football stadium, and every other weekend would pass fans streaming down the hill to the game. I'd see them coming back up the hill after the final whistle. The remarkable thing was that, unless you'd been following the match yourself, you'd never know whether they'd won, drawn or lost. You'd have thought you could guess from their expressions, from the hang of their shoulders, what sort of afternoon they'd had, but you couldn't. Not even the snatch of a song or a chant could tell you for sure. They didn't look happy, they didn't look sad. They looked like what they were – fans.

Kevin Keegan enjoyed in his career a level of success few players could dream of emulating. He was central to one of the most illustrious eras of any club in the modern game, and he had the silverware to show for it. He was King Kev, Mighty Mouse, Special K. And yet there hangs over the second act of his life a halo of failure, a feeling that he blew it. That he should contain these extremes is what I find strange, and moving, and is partly why I wanted to write this book. But it's also because Keegan was a pioneer. He saw ways to turn the game to his advantage long before the days of super-agents. He negotiated his own contracts, secured sponsorships, even arranged his own transfers. In an age when footballers were still under the thumb of chairmen and directors, Keegan was out on his own as a businessman. Driven and restless, he was always plotting his next move. A self-motivator, he took on roles as if he were running Kevin Keegan plc – his own trainer, his own agent, his own chief executive officer.

The energy was as overpowering as the ambition. It was almost as if he didn't need anybody else.

I have never met Kevin Keegan and I didn't try to contact him for this book. I imagine he would have turned down requests for an interview. Talking to him was not an imperative in any case. He has lavishly retold his story in three autobiographies, each spaced roughly twenty years apart: *Kevin Keegan* (1977); *Kevin Keegan: My Autobiography* (1997); and *Kevin Keegan: My Life in Football* (2018). I have occasionally quoted from all three, but for the most part this is a portrait of Keegan coloured by my own memories, interests, judgements, digressions. As a lifelong fan of Liverpool FC and a particular devotee of English football in the 1970s, I hope that what comes across is my respect for him and, taken all in all, my admiration.

1
THE PLAYER

E ven prodigies need a patron, and no footballer ever had a patron like Bill Shankly. Manager of Liverpool since 1959, Shankly had transformed Anfield into a powerhouse and a place to be feared. By 1970 he found the team in a slump. His star players were ageing, motivation was wanting, and in February Watford had dumped them out of the FA Cup. A rebuild was urgently required. Andy Beattie, an LFC scout, had spotted 'a boy at Scunthorpe' with huge potential, but they would have to be quick. Preston North End had already put in an offer for £27,500, and there was also keen interest from Arsenal and Millwall. Shankly's assistant, Bob Paisley, who had watched Keegan a few times, advised the boss to buy him before someone else did. The Scunthorpe manager Ron Ashman was so eager to close the deal – in May 1971 Liverpool's offer of £33,000 was a fortune – that he personally drove Keegan to Anfield. They arrived at the ground to be told that the manager and chairman would see them shortly. Time ticked by, and while they waited

Keegan rested on a dustbin. A photographer happened to catch the moment, and as he snapped away Keegan joked about the 'right rubbish' the club was signing these days.

Shankly knew better. At the medical, when his new recruit stripped to the waist, he noted admiringly the lad's bantam physique (Shankly had boxed while in the RAF). At Scunthorpe Keegan had created his own maniacal fitness regime by running up and down the terraces carrying weights, and was now 'built like a tank'. The only hiccup to the transfer came when they sat down to talk money. Shankly was offering him £45 a week, but Keegan, his dad's advice tolling in his head ('Don't sell yourself cheap'), had a disappointed air. He claimed to be already on a decent wage at Scunthorpe. Shankly asked him whether £50 a week would be acceptable, and the deal was done. The raw recruit, still only twenty, knew his own worth. From that point on he would run his affairs and look after his money with a shrewdness not common among footballers.

At that time it was customary practice at Liverpool for new players to be given a turn in the reserves before they graduated to the big time. Keegan, almost unprecedentedly, was fast-tracked to the first team and made his debut against Nottingham Forest in August

1971. He scored after 12 minutes, and LFC ran out winners, 3–1. He had instantly started a buzz around the club. Shankly called him 'the inspiration of the new team'. Looking back now, one imagines he felt the way Martin Scorsese did on casting Robert De Niro as Johnny Boy in *Mean Streets*. The presence of a volatile and brilliant newcomer not only lends lustre to your project, it tends to energise everyone involved and makes them raise their game. Mark Hughes in his autobiography said that when Manchester United signed Eric Cantona in 1992, it gave the club more than a lift: the players were so impressed by their new star that they tried to copy his best tricks.

By the age of twenty-one Keegan was Liverpool FC's talisman and the engine of their dominance. He had also made his debut for the national team. He wasn't Britain's first-ever superstar footballer: George Best had got there before him. 'I wanted so much to have his ability,' Keegan admitted in an interview. But Best, for all his electric brilliance, never had the ambition that drove Keegan. Indeed, he became the anti-Keegan, wilfully trashing his legend in a sybaritic haze of birds'n'booze'n'betting. He didn't care what people thought of him. Best's philosophy, if it could be so called, aligned with Viv Savage's of Spinal Tap, namely, 'To have a good time . . . all the time.' In any event, at the point of Keegan's flourishing in 1972 Best's fortunes had peaked and he had walked out on United for the first time.

It was clear from the way Keegan played that competitiveness was his lifeblood. You could see the lightning rods crackle from his perm. His sense of self was so deeply linked to his prowess on the field you almost feared for him. There is a price to be paid for wanting something too much. Shankly once told him before a game, 'Just go out there and drop some hand grenades' – encouragement that chimed with his explosive quality as a performer.

Explosive fitted not just his turn of pace but his temperament. Ripple-dissolve to Leeds vs Liverpool in the Charity Shield at Wembley, 1974, the season's 'curtain-raiser', which would now be utterly forgotten but for the spectacle of Kevin Keegan and Billy Bremner being sent off for fighting. Only days before, Keegan had been dismissed in a friendly against Kaiserslautern for lamping an opponent, so you might have thought he'd be on his best behaviour for the next game. But 'Dirty Leeds' had started at their most niggly, and despite Liverpool's complaints to the referee their fouling went unpunished. Johnny Giles had already clobbered Keegan ('That looked very much like a right hook,' cried Barry Davies on TV), then doubled down with a lunging tackle on him. In the melee that followed Bremner squared up to Keegan, who took a swing at him. 'I deserved to be sent off,' was Keegan's verdict, though at the time he was so angry he tore his shirt off as he left the pitch. It was a strange, almost gladiatorial thing to do (that bantam physique!), and the incident was soon blazed across the front pages as well as the back. By accident or design Keegan had made his dismissal one of the most famous in football.

The FA decided to make an example of the pair. They were both banned for 11 games and fined £500 each. Keegan was in disgrace, and yet I wonder if deep in his psyche he might have relished his sudden notoriety. Oh, of course it set a *terrible* example to youngsters, had brought the game into disrepute, blah, blah . . . but in terms of the Keegan brand it was far from a disaster. There was a bit of devilry in the lad after all. Never one to let slip an opportunity, Keegan used the enforced lay-off to bring forward his wedding day. He and Jean got married on the sly in Doncaster on 23 September 1974, thus evading the fans and denying the newspapers a day out.

Keegan's relationship with the media was ambivalent. On the one hand, he wanted a private life for his own and his family's sake. On the other, he saw the value of keeping in with the people who shaped his public reputation. Yet he couldn't always help himself. The heart and the head were at war within him, and it was never an equal contest. It was notable that after the Wembley dismissal he kept a much tighter rein on his temper. In the three years that remained of his Liverpool career he was never sent off again. Considering how often he was targeted by defenders in the mid-1970s – and how little protection flair players were given – that counts as an achievement in itself.

It wasn't until he was playing in Germany that he next got his marching orders – in a friendly. What was it about friendlies that triggered him? A friendly is a game that doesn't matter. But every game mattered to Keegan. In December 1977 Hamburg had scheduled a match against Lübeck, who greeted Keegan with a bouquet of flowers in acknowledgement of him coming second in the European Footballer of the Year awards. The gesture proved a false flag. Within seconds of kick-off Keegan's marker, Erhard Preuss, flattened him, out of sight of the referee. Minutes later he was viciously upended by a tackle: same player, same non-intervention by the ref. The third time Preuss tried to block him Keegan stayed on his feet, and when the defender laughed, Keegan delivered a haymaker – 'the hardest I had hit anyone in my life'. Preuss stayed down, and for a horrified second Keegan was afraid he 'might have killed him'. He hadn't – but he did get sent off. As well as a fine and a three-game suspension, he was obliged to return to Lübeck and apologise to their fans, which was the etiquette in Germany.

But what he was doing at Hamburg anyway? In the summer of 1977 Keegan was the most sought-after footballer in Britain. He had just helped Liverpool clinch a famous league and European Cup double, and could have gone on to burnish his name in the golden fields of Italy or Spain. Instead he chose Hamburger SV, who had finished sixth in the Bundesliga that year. In his autobiography he admits that he knew very little about the club. In fact, he was waiting for a scheme to work itself out. A year earlier he had inserted a clause in his contract with LFC that allowed him to leave for a fee of £500,000 – a relative steal. He knew that the lower the transfer fee, the more likely a prospective club would be to bump up his money.

At the time the deal raised eyebrows – his salary would be £100,000 a year, more than four times what he was paid at Anfield. Among the fans the idea got about that Keegan was a mercenary. The man himself would argue, not unreasonably, that he was being paid what he was worth. But fans are always looking for a grievance. Some even claimed that Keegan in his last season had lost the aura of old, back in the years when he was playing for Shankly. A player known to be on his way out of a club risks the wrath of the diehards. It so happens I was at Anfield for Keegan's final league game, a 0–0 draw against West Ham in May 1977, and I don't recall a moment to suggest his mind was elsewhere (he came closest to scoring, too, when a shot of his hit the post).

After an edgy start at Hamburg, where certain players resented the newcomer and his stratospheric wage, Keegan gradually settled. He won the fans over and earned himself the nickname of 'Mighty Mouse'. In his second season the club won the Bundesliga, and Keegan himself won European Player of the Year in both 1978 and 1979, an astonishing tribute at a time when his Continental peers included Beckenbauer, Cruyff and Platini.

It was doubly astonishing, when you remember that Keegan's international career coincided with England's dead-duck era of the 1970s. He had made his debut in November 1972, against Wales, in the faltering last days of Alf Ramsey's reign. Keegan understood the honour of playing for Ramsey, though he was selected for the team only sparingly. His precocious image perhaps militated against him, and his flair surely did – Ramsey had a lifelong suspicion of the gunslinger type with his tricks and flicks. Keegan was named as a substitute in the fateful World Cup qualifier against Poland at Wembley in October 1973, when the Polish goalkeeper, Jan Tomaszewski, proved England's nemesis. With minutes to go at 1–1 and England desperately seeking a winner, the call came down the bench for 'Kevin' to get changed. Keegan was ready to go on when another shout came – it wasn't him, it was Kevin Hector that Ramsey meant.

The result was a draw, England had failed to reach the World Cup finals, and by the spring of 1974 Ramsey was gone. His dismissal and the retirement of several old-guard players opened the door for Keegan's full-time return under caretaker manager Joe Mercer. It was a happy union. In his autobiography, Keegan said he warmed to Mercer's footballing philosophy ('a game of pleasure') and admitted that it was something he later tried to emulate: 'I probably carried into my management career more of Joe Mercer than of any other manager I knew, including Bill Shankly.' It was an approach that valued style and spontaneity over the 'deep-thinking' school of coaching. The passage is instructive, and illustrates a blind spot in Keegan's vision: because he was an instinctive player who didn't require much coaching he couldn't quite understand why anyone else would need it. He had taken to heart

Shankly's line that football was 'a simple game complicated by coaches'. But that was just Shankly exhibiting
his knack for a soundbite: *he* knew the value of coaching, just like the rest of the Boot Room at Anfield did.
We will see, in time, where that misunderstanding of
Keegan's led to.

The appointment of Don Revie as England manager
was a boon to Keegan, despite his initial misgivings.
Revie's management of Leeds, then the most unpopular
club in England, had earned him a reputation as a cynical pragmatist. But the two of them got on from the
start, and Revie's improvement of the England match
fees – £200 for a draw, £300 for a win – would have
endeared him to a money-conscious player. He also
gave Keegan a second chance after a serious falling-out.
In May 1975 England were due to play Northern
Ireland in Belfast, at the height of the Troubles. The
FA had received a death threat, and Keegan was the
target. Revie suggested he sit the game out, but Keegan
insisted on playing. He would later quote the match
reporter who reckoned that on the night the player
had run around a lot without much impact. A fair cop,
said Keegan, who had kept running in the belief that 'a
moving target would be harder to hit'.

When he was left out for the game against Wales the
following week, Keegan went into a sulk, packed his

bags and left the team hotel. It was an early sign of his petulance and tendency to storm off when things didn't go his way. Back home he soon realised his mistake, and once Revie phoned to explain his decision (he wanted to save him for the important game against Scotland three days later), Keegan climbed down and returned to the squad. Ramsey wouldn't have been so understanding. Just how thoroughly his walk-out was forgiven is evidenced by the fact that Revie made him captain the following year. Yet the England team never thrived under their partnership. Results were poor, and after another mediocre World Cup qualifying campaign in 1977 Revie quit the job for the money pots of the United Arab Emirates. It was a back-door move and damned by all as a betrayal. Almost all: Keegan reckoned Don was 'a quality person', not a money-grabber at all, despite selling his story to the *Daily Mail* for £20,000.

England would miss consecutive World Cups, but for Keegan there was a silver lining. He went on record to say that captaining his country was the greatest honour of his career, greater than anything he had achieved at club level, even the European Cup win. Eh? One can't imagine any other Liverpool player making such a claim, even if they thought as much. The fans wouldn't stand for it. What could be more important than playing for Liverpool? Certainly, he carried the England colours with honour, and there were brilliant goals among the 21 he scored: brave headers (he was always brave); a magnificent chip against Ireland at Wembley in 1980; against Scotland the one–two he played with Trevor Brooking before sliding it beneath the advancing goalie. And yet luck and judgement conspired against him even when the scene was set fair for national success.

His first game as captain came in 1980 at the Euros in Italy. The eight-team format looked helpful, with two groups of four and the winners advancing to the final. England were drawn with Spain, Italy and Belgium. In May at Wembley they had hosted a friendly against World Cup winners Argentina, featuring a nineteen-year-old Diego Maradona, and won 3–1. A gruesome photo op with Keegan and Emlyn Hughes kissing Mrs Thatcher (holding a football) on the steps of Number 10 felt a more ambiguous blessing. In Turin, England's first game, against Belgium, a 1–1 draw, was completely overshadowed by violence on the terraces. Police fired tear gas into the crowd. The pictures of rioting fans were beamed to TV audiences across Europe. English football hooliganism, having defiled the domestic scene, was suddenly our most famous export. Interviewed after the game, Keegan said he was 'ashamed to be English'. Manager Ron Greenwood echoed his sentiments: 'We have done everything to create the right impression here, then these bastards let you down.'*

Three days later, England, now international pariahs, were not in the best frame of mind to face Italy. Hard to play in front of fans you're ashamed of. They lost 1–0 to a late Marco Tardelli goal.† Keegan, struggling with a knee injury, never got going, though he almost equalised late on with an overhead kick. The team went to Naples and beat Spain 2–1, but it was too late to stop unfancied Belgium winning the group. England returned home to the howling execrations of the media. In his 1997 autobiography Keegan omits to

* The problem of hooliganism had been noted by Keegan during his appearance on *Parkinson* in October 1979. His fellow guests that evening were Lorraine Chase and Kenneth Williams, the latter confiding in his diary that Keegan was 'excellent & dishy'. In a discussion about violence around the game, Keegan said that footballers weren't to blame: 'Quite honestly, it's a lack of education. I think the football pitch is used as a battleground for it.' 'Yes, precisely,' Williams agreed. Nowhere in his autobiographies does Keegan make mention of Williams, or Chase, or indeed Parky.
† Who on scoring did a test run for his Greatest Goal Celebration Ever two years later in the 1982 World Cup final vs Germany, arms in strongman pose, face a Munch mask of delirious warrior-triumph. Keegan's goal celebrations were also distinctive: a double donkey-kick with fists raised to his chest, boxer-style, then a kid's leap into the grateful embrace of a teammate.

mention the tournament altogether, as if it never happened. He jumps from England's failure to qualify for the 1978 World Cup to Ron Greenwood's 'unremarkable' first seasons as manager, when the national side 'did not really come under the microscope' . . . Sorry? Did he just forget about the horror show in Italy?

England at last qualified again for a World Cup, the 1982 tournament in Spain, and began in fine style by beating France and Czechoslovakia. Keegan, now thirty-one, didn't play in either game, having inflamed an old back problem, and nor did Trevor Brooking, also recovering from injury. It's said that Keegan's presence unsettled the England camp; he didn't hide his dissatisfaction and kept apart from the others, like Achilles sulking in his tent. In the end he made the extraordinary decision to travel to Germany to see a specialist he trusted. Ron Greenwood wanted the trip kept secret from the press, so Keegan left the team's Bilbao hotel in the dead of night to drive himself to Madrid for a dawn flight to Hamburg (a hotel receptionist had lent him her Seat 500). He got his treatment and returned within 48 hours, but probably exacerbated his back trouble with the driving. It says much of the player's desperation to get fit. Putting himself through such an ordeal says even more about his strangeness. He was stranger than he knew – than any of us knew.

England had drawn o–o with West Germany in Keegan's absence and now needed to beat Spain by two clear goals. Greenwood had a dilemma: stick with the team that had got England this far or risk fielding Keegan and Brooking, uncertain of their match fitness. He left them on the bench, a decision Keegan in his autobiography calls 'Greenwood's biggest mistake'. He reckoned that even in the final 18 minutes when they came on as substitutes England might have got a result. 'We were his two best players,' he claimed, and, more arguably, they were 'definitely fit'. In the event both players had a chance to score. Keegan's was more or less an open goal, from a Bryan Robson cross, but somehow he screwed his header wide – possibly the most famous miss of the 1980s. o–o it stayed. England were out of the tournament without having lost a game.

It proved to be his swansong on the international stage. When Bobby Robson, the new England manager, announced his first squad for a European Championship qualifier against Denmark in September 1982, Keegan wasn't in it. A bombshell for everyone, not least the man himself. At thirty-one he might have sensed the shadows were getting longer, but his self-belief burned ever bright. Years later, the disappointment still rankled. He claimed that it was the manner in which Robson discarded him that hurt. The news of his exclusion had come via the press: 'I felt I deserved a phone call . . . It would have cost Bobby Robson ten pee to phone me up at Newcastle.' Strange that even a phone call is costed in Keegan's universe. Though I like the idea of an England manager sidling into a public phone box and checking his pockets for a coin to call his star player.

It's possible that Robson had been tipped off by Don Howe about Keegan's volatility. Howe, Ron Greenwood's right-hand man, had once seriously offended Keegan by insulting his friend Brooking. In an off-the-cuff comment about Brooking's failure to track back, Howe clumsily referred to him as 'cheating'. He had to apologise since 'the lads were in uproar', Keegan recalled, and you can bet who was leading the charge. You notice this disputatious side of his nature particularly with managers. He clashed with the coach at Hamburg over his punitive training regime. He clashed with Brian Clough, who, despite once trying to sign Keegan, would wind him up whenever the chance arose.* (Brought together as TV pun-

---

* Shankly on Clough: 'Like the rain in Manchester, though the rain in Manchester stops sometimes.'

dits for the 1978 World Cup they traded petty and silly insults about patriotism.) He clashed with Bob Paisley, who, after Keegan had gone to Hamburg, gave it as his opinion that players earning their living abroad shouldn't be allowed to represent England. He clashed with his manager Lawrie McMenemy at Southampton when he called the team 'cheats' for not playing well. This was a trigger word for Keegan: 'No one could accuse me of cheating on a football field.'

That he was playing for Southampton in the first place was barely credible. The story went that McMenemy had heard that Keegan's contract at Hamburg was up at the end of the season and got hold of his number. He called Keegan on the pretext that certain lights he was after for his new house could only be purchased in Germany – Hamburg, in fact. The two had a conversation, and a deal was soon in the offing. (Was this really how transfers were done back then?) It's all the more baffling when one considers that Juventus were favourites to get his signature at the time. Keegan says that his wife wanted to move back to England, and in any case he loved the New Forest and the idea of settling down there near his mate and horse trainer Mick Channon. But also significant was Hamburg agreeing to a maximum fee of £500,000, just as Liverpool had done three years earlier.

He repaid McMenemy's faith in him, scoring 30 goals in his second season, 26 of them in the league, and winning the Golden Boot. At the end of January 1982 Southampton topped the table, and for a while it seemed they might be on the verge of an incredible triumph. Keegan reckoned the team needed reinforcements, and told the boss so. McMenemy claimed not to have the funds, the club's title challenge collapsed, and the star player became disillusioned. Nevertheless, Keegan said he learned more in two years at the Dell than he did in six at Anfield, notably 'that clubs like Southampton cannot be champions of England'. Did that really come as a revelation to him?

At Southampton he also played alongside his old England teammate Alan Ball, then in his late thirties. Keegan was a sincere admirer as well as a friend, and in his autobiography expressed regret that Ball hadn't been more successful as a manager. Here is his interesting diagnosis: 'If he had a fault in his management style it was that he had too much passion.' You'd laugh at the cheek, if he wasn't deadly serious. He goes on to identify Ball's particular failing as manager of Manchester City, where 'he wanted to be the players' friend but demanded too much of them'. He might have taken heed on that score, but, being Keegan, he didn't see it.

*

Following the sojourn at Southampton and the huge dis-appointment of England's World Cup of 1982, Keegan needed a pick-me-up. Ron Atkinson at Man Utd had been checking his availability, but once Newcastle boss Arthur Cox got in touch the next move was a foregone conclusion. Keegan now had the chance to join the club his late father had supported, and what better way to honour the old man's memory? At that point Newcastle had been in the Second Division for four years – the verb 'to languish' is commonly preferred here – but the club could afford him because Keegan, typically, had nailed down a clause in his Southampton contract that specified a maximum transfer fee of £100,000.

It was the mothership calling him home. He ven-erated the 'passion' of the club, though he'd noted the falling-off of attendances at St James's Park. In Newcastle's last home game of the 1981–82 season against Wrexham the gate was under 10,000 – unthink-able today. Keegan knew the buzz around him would bring in the crowds, and struck a deal accordingly. He would get 15 per cent of the receipts from gates above 15,000, a transaction kept secret lest it unsettled the other players. It was shrewd, though even Keegan was surprised by the subsequent leap in weekly atten-dances. It brought in so much money he admits he was 'embarrassed' . . . but not so embarrassed that he didn't enjoy 'dreaming it up, negotiating it and seeing it work'. Once again, he was ahead of his time in the business of personal marketing.

Newly appointed captain, Keegan was initially dismayed by the unimaginative lump-it-and-run tactics of Cox's team. Even with Terry McDermott and a young Chris Waddle in the side Keegan realised promotion was a vanishing prospect. As his biographer Ian Ridley pertinently remarked, 'Keegan may have been wondering if he, like the *Titanic*, should never have left Southampton.' Newcastle finished fifth that season, three points short of promotion, though it might as well have been 33. Keegan, sharing spokesman duties with Cox, told the press that recruitment at the club needed to improve, 'as much for the benefit of the fans as myself'. Invoking the fans was a clever way of telling the board it had to step up. The captain wasn't prepared to let the ship drift.

His fighting talk paid off. In the 1983–84 season Cox brought in Glenn Roeder, plus a new goalkeeper, two full-backs and a young Tyneside striker who'd been playing in Canada named Peter Beardsley. His career hitherto had not been noteworthy, and Keegan for one was sceptical when the lad showed up at St James's Park looking like 'a bloke off the street who had won a competition to train with us for the day'.

Appearances . . . At his first training session Beardsley shocked them all with his skill, energy and vision. His goals would have a catalytic effect on the team. But he also mucked in with the groundsmen, put out the training cones, did the odd jobs. If they were short of a goalie in pick-up games, Beardsley would volunteer to go in. Maybe he reminded Keegan of his own boyhood love of 'keeping, throwing himself around.

Keegan likened his protective role with the younger players to 'the general in the trenches with the troops' – a fundamental misunderstanding of where a general in wartime would position himself. He had signed on for another year at the club, though it was an unforeseen moment on the pitch that would prompt his next dramatic decision.

It came at Anfield, strangely enough, during a third-round FA Cup tie in January 1984. Keegan's Newcastle arrived as underdogs and endured a cur's whipping, 4–0. During the game Keegan pushed the ball past Mark Lawrenson, intending to go on a run, just as he'd done against defenders hundreds of times before. This time was different: Lawrenson easily outpaced him and took the ball himself. The moment stunned Keegan like a *coup de vieux*: 'Nothing like that had ever happened to me before,' he recalled. He knew, instinctively, it was the end.

A month later, on his thirty-third birthday, he announced his impending retirement. Having clinched third place and promotion in May, Newcastle staged a farewell match for him at St James's Park against Liverpool. It ended in a 2–2 draw, the home team's scorers Keegan from the penalty spot and McDermott with a screamer. All the profits would go to the club, Keegan very publicly insisted, as a war chest for next season. Yet all that anyone remembers about the afternoon was his exit from the ground – by helicopter. There was something at once heroic and faintly absurd about the spectacle of Keegan, still in his kit, taking his leave after a final wave in the centre circle. Up, up and away into the clouds. It felt very 1980s as a *sayonara*. The Last Action Hero was quitting town. And, inconceivably, he was quitting football.

2
THE NORTHERNER

Keegan once described himself as 'the mongrel who made it to Crufts', and it's true that his mixed identity encompasses three different strains of northerner: where his family came from, where he grew up and where he made his name. Tyneside, Tykeside, Merseyside: a potent trinity. He was born on 14 February 1951 in the mining village of Armthorpe, South Yorkshire, at his Aunt Nellie's house. His home was a terrace, Spring Gardens, in the middle of Doncaster, and by his own account nested within the mythological dark of northern hardship: no electricity, no inside toilet or bathroom, the house lit by gas mantles and fuelled by coal. Outside their door trams heaved by, and the Co-op Funeral Services stood across the road as a memento mori. It was a domestic existence that hadn't changed since before the war – the First World War.

His father, Joe, was a miner who had moved to Yorkshire from Stanley, near Newcastle, where his own father, Frank, had worked in the Burns coalfield. Keegan recalls with pride his grandfather's heroic rescue work on the day of a pit disaster in 1909, when 30 from a workforce of nearly 200 were saved (the ages of the dead ranged from thirteen to sixty-two). Joe left the north-east when work became scarce, though he took with him his love of Newcastle United and handed it on to his older son. Kevin's birth year coincided with the first of Newcastle's trio of FA Cup wins that decade: against Blackpool in 1951, Arsenal in 1952 and Man City in 1955. The striker Jackie Milburn was a sacred name in the Keegan household.

Kevin's two closest boyhood friends, David and Maurice, were notably better off than his own family. They lived in houses that had electricity and television, the latter an unimaginable luxury at that time. We can picture the young Kevin staring at the football on the box and making a hero of the Wolves and England captain Billy Wright, small of stature like him, but with a mighty heart. Kevin was too short even to be a newspaper boy – he couldn't reach the letter boxes – so he earned pocket money by cleaning cars and collecting wooden crates from the market to break up as firewood and sell in bundles. Family days out were at Doncaster races, home of the St Leger, where he conceived a lifelong passion for horses.

It was a win at the races that enabled Mr Keegan to buy his son his first pair of (second-hand) football boots. This in spite of a doctor who, diagnosing croup in the lad's chest, advised his mother not to let him play sports at all. Keegan began to hone his talent – as a goalkeeper. He liked to throw himself about, making saves and muddying his togs so badly he was too filthy to be let on the bus. His local Catholic school, St Francis Xavier, employed no sports master, so football practice was taken by the headmistress, Sister Mary Oliver, who became the first significant influence on his career. In her black habit she cut a striking figure on the pitch, and her refereeing brooked no dissent: 'We could never argue with the decisions for they were clearly coming from the very top,' Keegan wrote, wittily. The tribute he pays to her memory is comparable only to the one he later pays Shankly. Sister Mary's example was one of Yorkshire can-do: she wasn't obliged to provide football coaching for her pupils, but she did so because she knew what a difference it might make. Keegan never forgot her.

School was not his métier, and though he passed his 11-plus he tended to fool around in class. One teacher remembered him as an exhibitionist. Lack of height may have been the motor for his clowning; as a small kid he was possibly too eager to get himself noticed. By now he had moved to St Peter's in Cantley, where his new football teacher realised that while the five-foot boy was eccentric enough to be a goal-keeper, he would never be tall enough. He switched him to play outfield, on the wing. Though greatly dis-heartened by his height, he had stamina and pace, and his skills got him a schoolboy trial at Coventry City, at that time managed by Jimmy Hill. Six weeks of training followed, and Keegan had made it to the last two – when the club let him go. He felt 'a complete failure', he says, though something must have spurred him onwards, some mixture of resilience, determina-tion and self-belief: he was Kevin Keegan, after all. Perhaps that same spirit prompted him as a fifteen-year-old to undertake a charity run from Manchester to Doncaster across the Pennines. Distance: 50 miles. Fifty. Miles. Out of his fellow runners he was proud to be the last one standing, or staggering, having reached Barnsley before his legs gave way. It's not quite *The Loneliness of the Long Distance Runner* – Keegan would never be Tom Courtenay's Borstal boy – but it chimes with his cussedness, the instinctive refusal to bend to anyone else's will.

He left school with two O-levels, in art and his-tory. His prowess as a footballer still unrecognised, he found a job as a tea boy in the unlyrical environs of Pegler Brass Works in Doncaster, on £6 a week. Here they manufactured taps, ballcocks, 'toilet fittings', everything, including the whole kit and caboodle. Does any combination of words sound more northern than 'Pegler Brass Works'? At this point you can't help picturing the slight teenager on the factory floor, daydreaming himself along like the romantics of 1960s kitchen-sink cinema – Tom Courtenay (again) in *Billy Liar*, Alan Bates in *A Kind of Loving*, Albert Finney in *Saturday Night and Sunday Morning*. His workmates were, in fact, mostly women, whose sense of humour (as he rather prudishly observed) was 'far cruder' than men's. His schoolboy banter perhaps turned out to be a punier defence than he supposed. That he neither drank nor smoked might also have been cause for teasing. It would have reminded folk that this lad was *in* the North but not necessarily *of* it.

Outside of work hours football was keeping him busy. At weekends he would play three times: for the Brass Works reserves on Saturday mornings, a youth club on Saturday afternoons and a pub team on Sundays. The pub was of no social interest to him – he had never set foot in the place – and yet it was via this association that he got his break. One Sunday he happened to be playing against Bob Nellis, a local scout with contacts at Scunthorpe United. Nellis was so impressed by the diminutive kid on the right wing that he asked him later if he fancied a trial at Scunthorpe.

Did he ever. After a handful of matches and a game at the Old Show Ground* with the first team, the club's manager, Ron Ashman, asked him to sign on as an apprentice. He was on his way. The weekly wage was £4 10 shillings, less than he was earning at Pegler, but he didn't mind about that. It wasn't as if he needed money for beer or baccy. All the same, it was one of the last times he would ever accept a drop in pay.

Professional football at last, but no exit from the hard-scrabble life. Training began at nine. Keegan's journey to Scunthorpe was twenty-five miles, which meant rising at six o'clock each morning, out by seven, two buses and then hitching a lift on a milk van or lorry for the last fifteen miles. The slog through the dark and the cold. Like some indigent farmhand out of Thomas Hardy.

Football was by no means the sum of an apprentice's life. His chores included laying out the kit, painting

---

* Scunthorpe's home from 1899. The name 'Old Show Ground' sounded elegiac even during its lifetime, like *The Last Picture Show*. It survived two major fires and featured Britain's first-ever cantilevered stand, built at the nearby steelworks – perhaps the one where Keegan himself would work. Following financial difficulties and a ban on wooden grandstands, the ground was sold to supermarket chain Safeway in 1988 and demolished. A Sainsbury's now stands on the site.

the turnstiles, cutting the grass and marking the white lines on the pitch. Had they not heard of 'grounds-men' in Scunthorpe? The one perk of this routine was the ancient club tractor upon which the apprentices secretly fooled around. They had great fun racing it, until the moment Keegan got behind the wheel, hit a bump and totalled the vehicle. Up in flames. He and his trembling companions were marched off to see the boss, fearing dismissal. Who could afford to replace a tractor? In fact, the manager merely bawled them out and levied a fine – 'a massive £5 each' – with dire warnings not to misuse club equipment again.

Money was always tight. Players still had to buy their own boots. When the team travelled to away games, it was by bus (no toilet facilities provided), and tedium was kept at bay with endless card games. Keegan would do a party piece as a ventriloquist's dummy, bounced on the knee of Tom Taylor, sports correspondent of the *Scunthorpe Evening Telegraph*. It says something of his good nature that he sent himself up in this 'little feller–big feller' routine. His teammates must have been grateful for the entertainment, especially when the fixture list sent them to far-flung grounds. One trip to Exeter required an entire night on the road; they got back home just as the milk was being delivered.

Aged seventeen, Keegan was given a wage increase, to £7, and the club also provided money for his digs. He found a room in a house – his landlady a Mrs Ruby Duce – whose previous occupant was the club's former goalkeeper, Ray Clemence, recently signed by Liverpool. Keegan made his league debut against Peterborough Utd, without distinguishing himself, and Scunthorpe lost. Once promoted to the first team he became determined to stay there. There was nothing he could do about his height (he eventually peaked at 5ft 7), but he noticed how a teammate, Derek Hempstead, put himself through an exercise programme, running up and down the ground's new stand carrying dumb-bells. Keegan began to join him in this regimen on the terraces, and gradually put on the muscle that Shankly would admire on the player's arrival at Anfield. This was before the days of fitness coaches. Keegan took to weights on his own initiative, and it paid dividends when opponents tried to knock him off the ball.

He was still the new boy, but his presence and energy on the right wing had begun to win admirers. When Arsenal came to the Old Show Ground for a League Cup tie in September 1968, they thumped Scunthorpe 6–1, yet the visitors saw something in Keegan they liked and asked him to join their youth team for a tournament in Africa. FA rules prevented him from going. Bobby Robson, then manager of high-flyers Ipswich Town, was among several managers who considered him. He took away a lukewarm impression of the lad – too small, and no better than what he'd got – but later admitted he should have bought him.

Keegan put his head down and worked even harder. In his first season he played 29 league games. In his second, 1969–70, he was an ever-present, playing 46; in his third, 45 – a remarkable testament to both his fitness and his durability. The English Fourth Division, with its soggy pitches and agricultural tackling, was no place for the faint-hearted. In that Granada TV interview, when Gerald Sinstadt asked whether defenders had roughed him up, he admitted, 'I've been kicked a lot 'n' that, but it's not as tough as I'd thought it'd be, to be honest.' In other words: *I can take it.* He liked playing for his club, he said, but quietly made clear his ambition: 'Youth honours, then England honours, if possible . . .'

He didn't want to hang around Scunthorpe the rest of his life. This was about more than limited opportunity. In his first year at the club he discovered that wages dropped in the close season. The £15 a week he earned playing was reduced to £10 in the summer. One can imagine how this arrangement maddened Keegan.

Ever wary of being underpaid, he took a temporary job plate-laying at a local steelworks. He had no idea what 'plate-laying' was, but it paid 25 per cent more than the summer wage at Scunthorpe, so he was in for six weeks. The job turned out to be back-breaking, and possibly dangerous. His boss, a huge Ukrainian bruiser, worked them to tatters in the morning, then gave them the afternoon off. In his autobiography Keegan identifies this as a moment of political awakening. It didn't matter to the workers if they produced a million tons of steel a week or half that. He saw in it the failure of nationalised industry: 'There was no incentive.' He would never admit to it, but do we detect here the earliest stirrings of the northern businessman as free marketeer?

His spell at the steelworks proved useful, however, when he and his mate Phil happened to visit the St Leger Fair. You can almost smell the vinegar on the fish and chips mingling with the scent of dried grass, beer and Player's No. 6. Two schoolgirls, Jean and Wendy, had just got off the waltzers, giddy with laughter; the boys, a couple of years older, introduced themselves. As they got talking Keegan was asked what he did, and said that he was at the steelworks. To have told them he was a footballer would have sounded 'too flash'. By this time he owned a Cortina, bought with help from his parents, and he offered the girls a lift home. They accepted, somewhat reluctantly – Phil and Kev perhaps looked too eager, too obviously 'out on the pull' – and when the car stopped at traffic lights in the town centre, the two lasses jumped out and went to catch a bus instead.

It is touching to think of Keegan in these early courting days, driving around the town or further off to Sheffield in search of entertainment, a junior version of *The Likely Lads*. A few weeks later at the Top Rank Ballroom, he and Phil bumped into Jean again, this time with another girl. Far from being aggrieved by her disappearing act in the car that night, Keegan regarded it as the conduct of a nice girl with 'a bit of class'. But there was confusion on this second encounter, because Phil liked Jean, and Kevin liked her mate, and for a while it wasn't clear who was going out with whom. This for me irresistibly recalls a monologue, 'Back Answers', by the great Lancashire comedian Robb Wilton,* about two mates – the narrator and Jim Lowe – who double-date twin sisters Maudie and Flo,

---

* Wilton (1881–1957), one of the last survivors of English music hall, was best known for his monologues featuring incompetent or pompous authority figures. A radio recording of him performing 'Back Answers' is available at https://www.youtube.com/watch?v=Nxbf5p5_qbo.

and eventually walk them up the aisle without knowing who's got whom:

> Jim said, 'Have you married Flo?'
> I said, 'Flo? I don't know – but what if I have,
> you've got one.'
> He said, 'I wanted Flo.'
> I said, 'Oh, is that so? Well, your only chance has
> just gone.'
> Jim said, 'Do you know that you married Flo?'
> I said, 'No, I don't know that I knew.'
> Jim said, 'You married mine, she's got ten
> thousand pounds!'
> I said, 'Well, never mind, she'll do.'

When Keegan later saw Jean in a school play, he realised that she was the one, and they began stepping out.
Too bad for Phil! It eventually dawned on Jean that
the short-legged, Cortina-driving Lothario was in fact
a professional footballer, which was funny because she
turned out to be a great fan of . . . George Best.

Secure in his choice, Keegan looked back in senten-
tious mood on the pitfalls facing the tyro footballer:
'It is vital for an impressionable youngster to be able
to make wise judgements.' He had seen players who
were battened on by a court of 'lackeys', on hand to

occupy their time and spend their money. Strength of character (such as his own) and a certain wariness around the company you kept were significant weapons in the fight against exploitation.

Staying put has its advantages. Safety, comfort, a cleaving to tradition are attractive even to the most footloose youngster. There is also the fear of leaving behind the environment that has sustained you, your family, your friends. Billy at the end of *Billy Liar* is given a chance to escape the pinched horizons of his northern town – the dreary job at the undertaker's, his benighted parents – and get on a train to London with his doe-eyed beatnik girlfriend, Liz.* He declines to join her, too deeply involved in the drama of his fantasy life to risk the chaos of real life.

Keegan knew he must move on. He would always be grateful to Scunthorpe. The club was run in a haphazard fashion, as so much of the game was back then, and it was doomed to stump around the foothills of the Football League. Yet those three years were an important rite of passage. They had helped him grow up, 'even if' – you can hear it rankles still – 'the money was better at Pegler Brass Works and Appleby Frodingham Steelworks'.

---

* That she is played by Julie Christie at her most adorable damns Billy for his tragic failure of appreciation as much as for his faintheartedness.

3
THE STAR

To understand the depth of Kevin Keegan's impact in the 1970s you have to bear in mind how unusual it was to see a footballer actively promoting himself as a brand. Being a devotee of *Shoot!* I used to read his column there, a slot that was rotated (as I recall) each week with fellow England stars like Alan Ball and Trevor Francis. In this Jurassic era before social media, a magazine column was the only way to get an angle on your hero's personality, a sense of them 'off duty'. Of course, I had no idea at the time that his column was ghostwritten, nor indeed what a ghostwriter was. In any case, Keegan had bigger fish to fry. You would also see him on TV, engaging in lame repartee with Britain's top boxer, Henry Cooper, in an advert for Brut 33 ('deodorant with muscle'), the Lynx of its day. There he was in a public information film, wearing his *Super Fly* outfit of checked jacket and flares as wide as teepees, explaining to a kid how to cross the road ('Keep your eyes open,' he tells him – useful advice in almost any context) as part of the Green Cross Code.

He also fronted Lyons Maid Goal! lolly ices, Grundig radios, Pirelli football slippers (whatever they were) and Patrick football boots.*

He had signed for Liverpool FC in the week they lost the FA Cup final to Arsenal. Not that he minded: in one unguarded moment during an interview he admitted he'd been cheering for the Gunners. His instant rapport with Shankly ('That day I met the man who was going to make me') was backed up by raves in the press. Danny Blanchflower in his *Sunday Express* column hailed the newcomer as 'something special', having already been tipped off by his manager: 'He's the greatest living English player,' Shankly had told him, with characteristic understatement. 'You should know that. Don't wait for the others. You get in first and say that.' If Keegan was eager to make his name, there seems to have been an equal determination in Shankly to help him do so. His Liverpool side in 1971 was somewhat becalmed. There had been

---

* Which I actually bought. Keegan's boots beguiled me. In the early 1970s, when every other player wore Adidas or Gola, Keegan wore Stylo Matchmakers, with their prominent white fins stitched on the upper. Later, he went off-piste again by choosing a tiny French bootmaker, Patrick, whose shoes had a double stripe slanted against the ankle. It singled him out, in the same way that Cruyff wore his Holland shirt with two stripes on the sleeve, while the rest of the team wore the Adidas three.

no trophy through the door in five years, and having offloaded Ian St John and Roger Hunt the front line was lacking a leader. When Keegan scored twice in a friendly against Southport, Shankly decided to pair him with John Toshack in a first-team-vs-reserves game at Melwood. Keegan scored a hat-trick, and Toshack got two. His full debut came against Forest on the first day of the 1971–72 season, and he never looked back.

As a regular he was earning £150 a week, plus bonuses – 'mega-money', as he called it. He dumped the Cortina and bought the car of his dreams, a Datsun 240Z, though he continued billeting at modest lodgings on Lilley Road. His room had been recently occupied (hello again) by Ray Clemence, who must have thought he was being shadowed. Towards the end of 1972 *Shoot!* profiled him in one of their brisk Q&As.*
We learned that Keegan already had a new car (a BMW 2002), his favourite food was 'mixed grill', his most difficult opponent was Norman Hunter of Leeds, and the person he would most like to meet in the world

---

* Which was the page I turned to immediately as a reader. Here was insight and information stripped down to a basic format. The usual answer to 'favourite meal' was steak and chips. As for 'most difficult opponent', I can't recall the name of the player who said, 'My wife.'

was – wait for it – Harry H. Corbett of *Steptoe & Son*. Under 'Miscellaneous Likes' he listed driving fast cars, swimming and tennis, and under 'Miscellaneous Dislikes' 'smoking' and 'girls who wear a lot of make-up' (an early warning there for Jean).

On the pitch he quickly established an understanding with Toshack, a player not hugely rated by Shankly but one whose presence seemed to galvanise Keegan. His knock-downs and flicks forged a near-telepathic connection with Keegan's movement, and goals flowed between them.* *Were* they in fact telepathic? I recall one peculiar occasion during the full flowering of their partnership when an early-evening news programme on Granada posed that very question and invited them

---

* A favourite of mine, against Leicester in an FA Cup semi-final replay at Villa Park, April 1974: midway through the second half, at 1–1, Toshack sees Keegan breaking down the middle and lifts a pass over the defence. Keegan, watching the ball as it drops over his shoulder, lob-volleys it over an advancing Peter Shilton. The timing, weight and delicacy of the strike are what make it extraordinary. I never saw anything to compare with it, until 16 years later, when David Platt scored in the last minute from a floated Paul Gascoigne free-kick against Belgium in Italia '90. Alessandro Del Piero scored a similarly spectacular dink-volley for Juventus to win a 1994 Serie A game 3–2 against Fiorentina. It's such a rare and difficult skill to master that you see these goals maybe once in a generation. The last one I recall was Robin van Persie's sensational volley from Wayne Rooney's long pass against Villa in April 2013. There may have been greater goals in the Premier League era, but I can't think of one.

to take part in an experiment. I was hopeful of scientific verification, but as the presenters arranged the pair back to back and asked them to guess, unseen, a sequence of colours and shapes, I began to wonder. Keegan went first, trying to mind-meld as Toshack held up his five different colours and shapes. He got one right. They switched around, Toshack now the guesser . . . and he nailed four out of five! The programme makers were delighted and hurried off to edit the results for that night's show.

Keegan recalls discussing this unlikely feat with Toshack afterwards. Was there perhaps something in this telepathy lark? Toshack in reply burst out laughing: the reason he 'guessed' the shapes and colours Keegan was holding was because he could see them in the reflection of the camera lens. And he would have got all five if Keegan hadn't held the fifth one too low for him to see. But if the theory was a bluff, it was true nevertheless that both players had good instincts. And they made one another look better.

Keegan would be the first to acknowledge that he doesn't rank alongside Pelé or Cruyff or Maradona. He made himself a star not through great natural ability, but by application and energy. No player worked harder at taking the talent he had to the absolute limit. For a small player he was brilliant in the air, he could read a game, he was astonishingly fit and had Herculean powers of recovery. He had a knack for scoring vital goals. He was a team player as well as an individualist. If his talent ever came in for criticism, he would simply point to the fact that he was European Footballer of the Year in 1978–79 and 1979–80. But he had some intangible extra quality, which was this: crowds loved watching him, no matter whom he was playing for. With Keegan around, you sensed something volatile in the air, the whiff of smoke and danger. He made things happen.

His timing was also spot on. In the early 1970s there was a vacancy for a star. George Best, in decline, described Keegan as 'lucky' and 'an average player who came into the game when it was short of personalities'. Then the *coup de grâce*: 'He's not fit to lace my boots as a player.'* That may have been true, but you also feel the needle of envy in that lofty judgement. Keegan was by then handling his career with a focus and diligence quite alien to Best's insolent waywardness. In terms of character and public perception the two players were very different. In his dark-eyed, snake-hipped devilry Best was Elvis,

---

* Nor, as sportswriter John Roberts remarked, was he fit to lace Best's drinks.

with the outlaw cheek to match. Clean-cut, ingenu-
ous, the boy you could take home to Mother, Keegan
was Cliff.

Maybe he liked that image, too. His first venture
into pop was a 1972 terrace stomper called 'It Ain't
Easy', with a chorus as catchy as a dose of the clap
('Believe me, it ain't easy / To live this life with me').
In his 1977 autobiography he recalls how the single's B-side, 'Do I Know You', was still being written
when he arrived at the recording studio. Jean had a
look at the lyrics, about a young man sleeping around,
and told him not to touch it. Sensible advice. 'I have
never looked for that kind of image and I never will,'
Keegan reflected, piously. The song was rewritten at
the last minute. The single sold pretty well, though
he deprecated it. When fans wrote to him saying they
couldn't get hold of a copy, 'I wrote back saying how
lucky they were.'

Later, playing for Hamburg in 1979 he was
approached by a couple of music-biz executives to
record a song, 'Head Over Heels', originally written
as a duet for Suzi Quatro and Smokie's Chris Norman.
Keegan thought it sounded a bit like Rod Stewart.
With his usual chutzpah he decided he could 'probably
get away with it', though he turned down the standard
industry contract – a percentage on sales – in favour of

a flat fee of £20,000. They paid it upfront. The single sold 220,000 copies in Germany, hovered around the top ten and was featured on a huge Christmas seller, *Franz Beckenbauer's Football Hits*. (Der Kaiser as pop impresario – who knew?) In the UK it reached no. 29, and Keegan went on *Top of the Pops* to perform it. You can watch him in all his permed glory on YouTube. He hasn't got a bad voice, though he looks a bit 'karaoke dad' with the gold chain and flyaway collars, and his concentrated gaze upwards during the guitar breaks makes it look like he's counting how many bars he should wait before the chorus. When the song was played on the radio for a slot called 'Smash of the Week', he was chuffed, until he realised the DJ had chosen it so he could smash the disc to bits live on air for being the worst record of the week.

The two music execs behind the song made, as Keegan carefully notes, 'a small fortune' out of it. But he concedes that they had taken the risk and so deserved the reward. In his autobiography he insists that the project was not just about making money anyway and that the experience was something that 'cannot be bought'. Which, coming from him, is quite the admission. The team got back together in 1980 for a second single, 'To Be Home Again in England', a misty-eyed folk dirge that once did service on *Family*

Favourites but otherwise made no ripple. Perhaps an early lesson there about attempting encores.*

With the money rolling in, he and Jean bought a farmhouse in North Wales – at last, a residence *not* previously occupied by Ray Clemence. The locale was a typically offbeat choice for Keegan, whose teammates tended to settle in the coastal enclave of Formby, north of Liverpool. A BBC team visited him one winter, with the house and surrounding acres under snow. He was happy there with his dogs and his horses. 'I love to be in the public eye. I like to be popular,' he said, but he also enjoyed 'the peace and privacy' of living in Wales. 'The people are farmers. They're not mad keen on football,

---

* Though it wouldn't be the last time we saw Keegan on *Top of the Pops*. Cut to May 1982, and the England World Cup squad reach no. 2 in the charts with 'This Time (We'll Get It Right)', a bewitchingly mediocre anthem written by the same duo behind 'Head Over Heels'. It didn't take long for the lyrics to ring hollow: 'To win them all / It's what we'll set out to do . . .' It was accompanied by a video of 'Ron's 22' in their Admiral sweaters, blokily knocking around the Abbey Road Studios. Keegan, front and centre in the recording booth, seems to be in command of the singing, while the others hold their lyric sheets, pretending to enjoy the moment. Phil Thompson reads from his with the frowning look of an examinee instructed to use both sides of the paper. The squad later appeared in the *TOTP* studio, miming to the single's atrocious flipside 'England (We'll Fly the Flag)', alongside stewardesses from British Airways – essentially a free ad for the company. Keegan, aka Andy McDaft, shows his 'fun' side by plonking on a stewardess's hat mid-performance. He looks like a friend of Noddy.

they're more keen on rugby. So I can talk to my neighbours and football never gets mentioned. That's quite nice sometimes.' The film reveals that he has now traded up to a red Range Rover, just then the ultimate badge of 1970s prosperity and great for those narrow, hedged lanes where you're likely to be stuck behind a tractor.

Probably the most famous of Keegan's non-footballing exploits was his epic performance on the BBC show *Superstars* in 1976. He put himself on a tight schedule back then. Having just helped LFC win the UEFA Cup against Bruges in May, he had 'eagerly accepted' the show's $500 fee, which nearly jeopardised the more lucrative £5,000 offer to play in a celebrity football match in Paris against the Brazilian Olympic team. The same weekend he had to travel back home to open a weekend fete at Rhyl (more glamour) and then get to Bracknell in time for the start of filming on *Superstars* on Monday. Talk about different times. The very notion of elite sportspeople risking their reputation on national telly to prove they were better at kayaking or weightlifting or table tennis is nearly inconceivable today. But back then Kevin Keegan wasn't going to pass up the chance of taking on Gilbert van Binst in a bike race.

It was the penultimate event, and Keegan was well positioned to win the overall competition. Van Binst, the Anderlecht captain, had brought along his own bike. Keegan's seemed to have loose wheels. They had made it to the corner when, trying to nip in front of the Belgian, Keegan clipped his rear wheel and went flying. *Sans* helmet, *sans* protective padding, he skidded across the cinder track. 'That is a terrible crash,' said commentator David Vine, and watching the incident on YouTube you can't help but wince. His shoulder and right arm were shredded and bruised. But you have to admire Keegan, who was brave to the point of nonchalance afterwards. 'It probably looks worse than it is,' he told Vine with a chuckle, and when the rerun was called he recorded the second-fastest time. Then he beat Ruud Kroll in the steeplechase – it's sport, but it's also comedy – and won the contest.

The drama didn't end there. After all the toing and froing, the early starts, the crash, he collapsed and had to be rushed to hospital in Northampton. He was on a drip for three days, diagnosed with a form of colic. He had earned his prize money ($2,000) a few times over. Not all of his peers took the contest as seriously. QPR's Stan Bowles* overturned his kayak and later

---

* Bowles (1948–2024) in the mid-1970s was as much a talisman at Loftus Road as Keegan was at Anfield, but notably different as regards application and attitude. Bowles loved to play, but he also loved to gamble, and the stories of his rackety lifestyle

accidentally blasted a hole through a table with a gun; he later attributed his ineptitude to having been out on the lash with James Hunt the night before. Now isn't that the best 1970s Brief Encounter of the Sporting Mavericks you've ever heard – Stan Bowles and James Hunt out on a bender? These were the glory days before the market went nuts, before agents blocked out the light and before anyone mentioned the word 'insurance'. *Superstars* was a hit (13 million watched it) at a time when sport on TV was mostly confined to *Grandstand* and *World of Sport*'s niche line-up of wrestling, speedway and cliff-diving. You can see why Keegan, fit and hungry for the spotlight, loved the

----

generally involved horses, dogs, tipsters, bookmakers, debt collectors, lost wages and visits from the bailiffs. He clashed with managers – Malcolm Allison, Tommy Docherty, Clough – and his total of five England caps speaks volumes about the national team's suspicion of gifted but wayward players in the 1970s. *Superstars* wasn't the only point of crossover between Bowles and Keegan. In 1977 Hamburg wanted to sign Bowles, ahead of their Liverpool target, and only the intervention of QPR chairman Jim Gregory with an offer of £4,000 cash persuaded the player to stay. Bowles's handling of sponsors reflected his happy-go-lucky philosophy. In his heyday he was contracted by Gola to wear their boots, payment, as usual, in cash. Adidas then offered him an enhanced deal of £250 per match, which he agreed to behind Gola's back. Bowles's teammates wondered how Stan was going to pull this off. The answer: the next game he wore a boot from each sponsor on either foot, thus doubling his money. Keegan had too much respect for his paymasters to have dared such a ruse.

show. He desperately wanted to go to the *Superstars* final in Florida, 'with the big appearance money', but Jean put her foot down. So too, presumably, did Bob Paisley.

By the middle of 1976 Keegan was restive and needed another challenge. Being a star he decided he must exit the stage like one. He announced his intention to leave Liverpool at the end of the next season. This was an unprecedented move at the time; the sale of a player was a transactional business between clubs, with no thought of a long goodbye. A twelve-year-old Keegan obsessive back then, I recall the moment like a punch to the head. It was far more shocking to me than the news of Shankly quitting. After all, managers were old guys, leaving was what they did. But Keegan was in his prime and beloved of the fans. What could he want outside of Liverpool, and where on earth would he go? This was the second shock. It wasn't just another club he was joining, it was another club *in Europe*. Say it ain't so, Joe!

Looking back, Keegan reckons that the seeds of his departure were sown when his great mentor left the club. Shankly had famously 'resigned' a number of times before, and the Anfield board had always persuaded him to stay. It was a kind of game they played. When in 1974 he announced his retirement, the club now took him at his word; there was no more begging him to reconsider. Thus unfolded the tragicomedy of the man who couldn't quite leave his greatest invention behind. Shankly began to turn up at Melwood, near his home, and join in the training. Inevitably, the players would address him as 'boss', which put the unassuming Bob Paisley in a horribly awkward position. Something had to give. Rumour got about that Shankly was no longer *persona grata* at the ground, and in high dudgeon he went off to train with Everton instead. Keegan bitterly blames the club for not just fudging the transition, but failing to honour the great man with a post-managerial role (life president would have covered it).

In any event the umbilical cord that held Keegan to the club had been cut. His dad had died in 1976, and with his surrogate father – the man who had made him a star – banished from the scene, he no longer felt beholden to Liverpool. Accusations of rank disloyalty were thick in the air around Anfield. But that didn't worry him: he knew his own worth, and how much he had given.* You can't help but wonder what might have happened if Shankly had still been at the helm.

---

* On a purely statistical basis, 323 games, 100 goals and a ton of assists.

Would Keegan have dared to leave? It's possible he might have hung on, sensitive to his debt of gratitude (and to a pinch of fear). He recalls with emotion the day of Shankly's funeral in 1981, some of the players in tears as they gathered in the front room, where his coffin lay. Pathos and comedy are in delicate equilibrium when he admits that, sadly, he was too short to carry the coffin and had to walk alongside it. The whole city came out to mourn Shankly, and when the funeral cortège passed the Bellefield training ground, the Everton players, still in their kit, stood there with heads bowed. 'It was one of the loveliest things I have seen in football.'

Before quitting the country, however, Keegan bequeathed one more thing to British life. I don't think we can call it a toxic legacy, though it did involve chemicals. It stands as a monument to the unlovely, the inglorious, possibly the indefensible. We need to talk about Kevin's perm. The 1970s are still called to account as The Decade That Style Forgot, but anyone with a modicum of taste knows that's wrong: the nadir of Bad Style is the 1980s. The perm straddled these decades. Keegan had already shown himself to be attuned to the fashion zeitgeist with his bell-bottom trousers, long-collared shirts and jackets with lapels as wide as bowling alleys. If he also wore Cuban heels, then that was at least tactical, lending him height. Glam rock was almost over by the mid-1970s, but one of its signature hairstyles, the poodle cut or bubble cut, had lingered on. Bowie, ever the pioneer, got a perm in 1969, the pre-Ziggy days, and got rid pretty fast. His friend Ian Hunter of Mott the Hoople shook his shaggy locks on *Top of the Pops*, but he was naturally curly-mopped and in his aviator shades made the exception to the rule: he looked cool.

Something was in the air – something chemical, which also required an afro fork comb to keep its shape. Just before Keegan left for Hamburg a hairdresser friend pointed out the advantages of permed hair: it was easy to maintain; you could 'wash and go'* and be halfway home to Wales while the other lads were still under the blow-dryer. One presumes that the hairdresser also said to him, 'You'll look good,' and managed to keep a straight face. Keegan's nickname at Liverpool was Andy McDaft, because, in his words, 'I didn't always get things right.' Hmm.

The big day came. Off he went to the salon, having arranged to meet Jean and his agent Harry Swales afterwards in a restaurant off Church Street, Liverpool.

---

* It's quite surprising that he never monetised this look with his own-brand shampoo.

The hairdresser in charge of his tonsorial transformation said it would require at least half an hour beneath the huge heated hairdryer. Keegan, running late for his wife, told him he didn't have time and insisted he dry it with a hand-held. Out on the street it must have felt like a tottering peruke had been clapped on his head. He entered the restaurant – and Jean and Harry fell about laughing. The latter noted his likeness to a Coldstream Guard. An emergency damping-down of the barnet in the loo yielded little change. Yet the ridiculous sight he presented didn't cow him, and instead of hurrying back to the salon (and thus sparing us a generation of poodle-haired madness) he styled it out, no doubt to the vast amusement of his teammates.

But those who come to scoff sometimes remain to pray, or in this case, to spray. Phil Thompson, LFC stalwart and a former teammate of Keegan, spotted a photo of the 'little guy' playing for Hamburg and evidently liked what he saw. As he recalls in his autobiography, *Stand Up Pinocchio*, he decided to take the plunge himself one Saturday and went off to Charlie Wynn's Chopping Block hair salon in Kirkby. He emerged hours before a League Cup tie against Wrexham at the Racecourse Ground. In the dressing room he got a lot of stick from the players, which was bad enough. When he ran out at kick-off, one can only imagine the Eisteddfod of derision that greeted him from the terraces. 'Look, Liverpool have signed Shirley Temple!' During the game, and perhaps for many games thereafter, it seemed that 'every time I got the ball, someone would shout, "Hit the big poofter!"'

His brave example did not go in vain. Soon, Phil Neal and Terry McDermott went the way of the perm; across Stanley Park at Everton so did Mick Lyons and Bob Latchford. Thompson remembered that as other players succumbed the whole conversation changed. Instead of 'All right, mate, how's the family?' it became 'How's the perm? Where did you get it done?' It wasn't long before the style was adopted by the fans, and the image of the 'tached-and-curly-haired Scouser took off. It spread to pop and TV in the 1980s via Peter Gill, aka Ped, drummer for Frankie Goes to Hollywood, and Brian Regan, who played Barry Grant's mate Terry Sullivan in the Channel 4 soap *Brookside*. From there it hardened into a regrettable stereotype, thanks to Harry Enfield's bewigged Three Scousers, who alternated fighting one another with a repeated injunction to 'Caaalm down!'

Does the blame fall entirely on Keegan? He had hightailed it to Germany before the trend really took hold. One could also point the finger at McDermott, who remained loyal to the perm-and-'tache combo for years, decades after, even as his greyed. Like those Japanese soldiers who hid out in the jungle, oblivious to the fact that the war had ended years ago, Terry Mac refused to listen when they said, 'It's over, mate.'

Keegan had put himself in an invidious position by announcing his departure so far in advance. Whenever he had an indifferent game the talk was that he had lost interest and couldn't wait to get away. If he played well, they said he was trying to court a buyer. The assumption was that he had already arranged his move, but in fact he was still in the dark as to where he would go even in April. He began to worry that he might be stuck in the shop window. Then an agent got in touch to get a deal going. At first Keegan thought he was bound for Bayern Munich, but it turned out that Hamburger SV wanted him and were prepared to pay £100,000 a year. Riches, and an unimaginable distance from the £50 per week he agreed with Shankly back in 1971. He signed for Hamburg in May 1977.

An anticlimax threatened to spoil his farewell. Liverpool had already secured the league title but had lost to Man Utd at Wembley in the FA Cup final. Keegan hadn't played well, and knew it. He and the team felt deflated, but they still had before them the prospect of a European Cup final. No other Liverpool side had ever come so far in the competition. The omens were good following an epic second-leg, quarter-final encounter against St Etienne in April. Keegan scored a sensational early goal from a cross that caught their keeper on his heels. David Fairclough clinched the tie with an even more memorable finish, earning himself the original epithet 'Super Sub'. In the final against Borussia Mönchengladbach we were 2–1 up when Keegan made his famous diagonal run into their penalty area that forced Berti Vogts, who'd been his shadow the whole game, to scythe him down. Phil Neal scored from the spot. As the Liverpool writer and academic Rogan Taylor nicely put it, 'The penalty was almost a kind of tribute from Vogts to Keegan.' The German went one better that night by turning up at the Liverpool team's hotel in Rome to share a drink and congratulate his nemesis. Keegan was greatly touched by this gesture of magnanimity from Vogts, perhaps all the more for knowing that he would never have done the same had their fortunes been reversed.

My dad, who'd been at the Stadio Olimpico that night, returned from Rome with a poster advertising the game. It hung on our kitchen wall at home for years. Whenever I looked at it I thought of Keegan and his swansong, and it gladdened my heart.

4
THE WANDERER

He wasn't the first famous son to have swapped Liverpool for Hamburg. In fact, the Beatles were unknown when they launched themselves on Germany, arriving in their manager's Austin van in late August 1960. The band – John Lennon, Paul McCartney, George Harrison, Stuart Sutcliffe, Pete Best – had not yet set the world, or even the Mersey, on fire. In the first three months of the year they had no professional engagements at all. They had also failed an audition to be Billy Fury's backing group. Their accommodation in Hamburg was squalid: two tiny rooms without electricity (one without a window), situated next to a toilet that served a cinema in the same building.

This first venture was not a success. They did a lot of drugs and slept with a lot of girls, but their stage performances weren't great. After chaotic residencies at two different clubs they fell out so badly with their employer that he had them deported after three months. In spring the following year they returned to

Hamburg and played 92 nights at the Top Ten Club between April and July. This was the environment in which they acquired their discipline and evolved as a group, clocking up the legendary 10,000 hours that Malcolm Gladwell in his book *Outliers* reckons to be the basis for mastering a skill. The talent was already there.

Keegan had completed his 10,000 hours long before he left Liverpool. We may assume it would have included 10,000 keepy-uppies, 10,000 sprints, 10,000 headers and, latterly, signing at least 10,000 autographs. At twenty-six he was probably in the best shape of his life and raring to go, buoyed up by an eye-poppingly lucrative contract. But his early experience of life in Hamburg was hardly more auspicious than the Beatles' had been. Partly, he was victim of his own success. If his teammates weren't already disgruntled by the open secret of his wages – higher than any other player in the history of the Bundesliga – they would have felt thoroughly affronted by the PR campaign the club's business manager, Peter Krohn, had organised around the new signing. Keegan was heralded as the saviour of and catalyst for the club, a fuss almost guaranteed to alienate the players who were already there. He soon felt the *froideur* on the training pitch, where no amount of arm-waving and pleading could get him a decent pass. This was something new for him – a bunch of teammates who seemed to hate his guts.

Outside the game, life wasn't much easier. The club had promised to find him and Jean a house, but for now they were billeted in a room on the 19th floor of the Plaza Hotel in Hamburg. The Keegans' two Old English Sheepdogs rather cramped the accommodation. In time the couple bought a bungalow in Itzstedt, a quiet village in Schleswig-Holstein that was much better suited to their taste for privacy.

Meanwhile, Krohn had hired an English-speaking coach, Rudi Gutendorf, whom the players liked no better than their perm-haired superstar. The atmosphere at the club had turned toxic by now, and all Keegan could do was keep his (enlarged) head down and play. In fact, his form was blameless, which attests to his professionalism and the tunnel vision at his command. However hostile the mood, he was single-minded about putting in a performance: he had never been one to hide. The lowest point came that December, when a two-legged Super Cup was held between Liverpool and Hamburg, a nightmare coincidence for Keegan, caught between old times and new. The first leg ended 1–1. The second leg at Anfield was a personal calamity as Liverpool cruised to a 6–0 victory, and the crowd, having welcomed back their prodigal son, took to crowing, 'You should have stayed at Anfield.' Just to rub it in, Kenny Dalglish, his replacement in the no. 7 shirt, was among the scorers.

Shunned by his teammates, misunderstood by the press, Keegan might have decided to chuck it all in and get out of town. What helped him through the rough times was the support. The Hamburg fans loved him and appreciated the effort he regularly put in, even under pressure. They could see with their own eyes what was happening on the pitch, where other players were denying him the ball. They kept chanting his name, and the little guy – 'Mighty Mouse', as he was affectionately known – answered their faith with good performances. Up in the boardroom they had seen enough, and change was afoot. Krohn and Gutendorf were shown the door, and in came Günter Netzer, one-time killer-blond midfield star of the 1970s West Germany side. Under his beneficent reign results improved, along with the team spirit, and a tenth-place finish in the Bundesliga reflected their hot-and-cold campaign.

Eager to get a foothold in his new place of work, Keegan had started to learn German. Such was his conscientiousness that even at home he and Jean would have evenings when they would speak only German to each other. In fact, their domestic life in Hamburg would get prolonged exposure when ITV shot a documentary, *Brian Moore Meets Kevin Keegan*, in the summer of 1979. It's fascinating for its casual insights into the Keegan lifestyle, but also for his unguarded views on money, marriage, pressure, ambition, politics. But mostly money. 'This house is worth £200,000,' he says of the large new-build bungalow that is home. The camera briefly focuses on the wrought-iron gates bearing the owner's insignia: 'KK'. 'When I left Liverpool, my last contract was worth £22,000 per year. When I signed for Hamburg, I was on £122,000 a year.' Admire the honesty. He and Jean are shown visiting their local supermarket, both of them talking in German to the assistants on the deli counter. 'I don't think there's much difference in the food,' he says. 'There's a definite difference in the price. Jean noticed that straightaway.' We're not in Kwik Save any more.

This is perhaps the first time we've ever heard Jean talking, and her sweet, soft-voiced, girl-next-door presence is very likeable. 'We're like really good friends,' says Keegan, as they sit together on the sofa. Evident fondness binds them, but also acceptance of a marriage built on conventional lines. He talks of giving Jean 'a hundred quid' to go and buy herself clothes. She will return with a skirt, two pullovers and 'ninety-two quid in change'. You detect his admiration for her thrift.

The film-makers follow him to an appointment with the fans – 'autograph hours', as the custom is known here. Keegan sits at a table while great shoals of fans, young and old, queue for him to sign photos, posters, memorabilia. It's like a book signing, without an actual book to sell. '£2,500 for an hour's work,' he comments, tickled by the idea of being paid to publicise yourself.

'I'm not really money-minded,' he says, unable at times to keep his mind on anything else. 'I don't think I could give you a figure for what I earn in a year. I could, if I really wanted to . . . but I don't really want to.' No matter, he's already admitted in the previous clip that he's now earning £400,000 a year at Hamburg. He knows he's a millionaire but keeps saying he doesn't think about it. 'We don't live like millionaires,' he adds. Cut to the interior of a private jet, Keegan in aviator shades talking earnestly to an odd-looking gent who with his moustache and wraparound sideburns bears a resemblance to the comedian Jimmy Edwards. This is in fact his business manager/agent Harry Swales, accompanying him on a PR trip to Patrick, his boot sponsors, at their HQ in France. There's a tender moment of Keegan on the factory floor, taking the hand of a middle-aged lady and planting a courtly kiss on her. Business doesn't preclude personal warmth, and the workers love him for it.

Before the camera's inquisitive eye Keegan talks with obvious self-consciousness about his new wealth. He enjoys it, but he doesn't want people to think it's changed him. As the plane's engines hum in the background, he says he's often asked to make personal appearances, most recently by Mrs Thatcher. He turned her down. Not, he explains, because he's anti-Tory but out of respect for his late dad, a socialist to his mining fingertips. Out comes a favourite family story about the old man's principles: one day the local Conservative Association asked Joe Keegan if they could use his house at Spring Gardens as a canvassing centre. His father promptly sent them packing, even though the fee, about £20, would have been riches to him. Keegan then spoils this filial reminiscence by admitting that the PM's request clashed with a game in any case.* Back on his sofa at home he's musing again on his money: 'It's not that I don't trust people . . . it's just that I don't trust people.' Even when he's trying to be discreet he can't help giving himself away.

He's somewhat defensive about Jean, who has to stay at home with their new baby daughter while he's away. At least she has the dogs for company. 'Substitutes for

---

* Nor would it stop him later sharing that photo op with Emlyn Hughes kissing Thatch on the steps of 10 Downing Street.

people,' he opines. 'Sometimes *better* substitutes for people.' Jean admits that he's not one for relaxing at home, that he's 'a very stubborn person – can be annoying at times'. As for the future, he tries to shield his cards, but can't resist giving us a peep at what's already on the table. Offers have come from Barcelona, from the US, from Saudi Arabia. This last again puts him in the vanguard, although he expresses scant enthusiasm at the thought of desert football: 'I wouldn't dream of taking my wife there for less than one million pounds a year,' he says, bizarrely. He would also be reluctant to make the move if it got in the way of representing England. 'That would probably be the hardest decision I'd ever have to make in my life' – in short, cash versus country – but the next minute he concedes it would be the 'easiest' decision, since he'd always want to play for England.

Wild scenes of Hamburger SV's Bundesliga win of 1978–79 close the documentary, with Keegan holding the trophy aloft on the balcony of Hamburg town hall, a vast gathering of fans below chanting his name. Perhaps this public adulation went to his head, for the interview ends on the potential bombshell that he'd like to get out of football in a couple of years and become . . . a politician. 'It really interests me. I'd love to have a bit to do with, well, our destiny. These people who've got so much power . . . I mean, I wouldn't just like to be a politician, I'd like to be prime minister. I'd like to have the power, you know?' Kevin Keegan, prime minister. Of all his ambitions this might be the most comical. And the most terrifying. Anybody less suited to the cynical, back-door churn of politics is hard to imagine. Though with his financial know-how he might have been a useful budget wonk at the Treasury. He would not have been one to crash the economy in, say, 49 days.

As European Footballer of the Year, Keegan could have gone anywhere he fancied, but with Hamburg now top dogs he decided to stay for a crack at the European Cup. This involved him making a deal with Netzer, now general manager at the club, so that he could play a summer in America for the Washington Diplomats. The incentive: he would collect £250,000 for four months' work ('This was some money for a lad from Donny'). Keegan was about to fly out on Concorde to sign the contract, when Netzer came to him with news of a serious hitch. Because of a recent rule change Keegan's employment in the States would make him ineligible for the next European Cup[*]

---

[*] Hamburg reached the final in 1980, only to lose 1–0 to Nottingham Forest.

until the semi-final stage. Another hard decision: Big Money or Big Cup? Keegan recalls that Netzer was 'very embarrassed' about the mistake, though he found a solution to the problem pretty quickly. He would pay Keegan the money he would have earned in the US on top of his regular salary. In other words, he was getting £250,000 for free. What's the German for *ker-ching*?

Not quite for free. In return Keegan would let the club and its sponsor BP use him as their face on TV and advertising. Opening shops and making personal appearances can be exhausting, of course, but it was still nice work, and Keegan knew it. With win bonuses on top it made him the best-paid player in Europe. Today such rewards would barely raise an eyebrow, but in 1979 he was football's first millionaire, its Rockefeller. He claimed to have never chased money since he blagged an extra £5 a week from Shankly, 'but it has always been there'.

As the canniest bargainer on the block he would not miss out.

What fields next to conquer? With his reputation burnished and his coffers full, Keegan was in the satisfying position of being able to pick and choose. He had proved himself a tough nut in Germany, surviving all that the Bundesliga could throw at him. Italy now played its siren song; he fancied learning the language and had no doubt the crowds would go mad for him. Talks with Juventus were already far advanced when he encountered a major snag: Jean didn't want to go. Hitherto in the story of Keegan's relentless rise to the top she had been a near-silent helpmeet, the supportive wife who cheered on her man but stayed out of the way. Keegan recalls that she feared Italy as a hotbed of terrorists and kidnappers, and it's true that the Red Brigades were bringing mayhem to the streets in 1980. But then so were Baader–Meinhof in Germany and the IRA in Britain. Nowhere felt that safe back then.

'You can go to Italy, but I am going back to England,' Jean told him in a forthright, challenging way that Keegan perhaps hadn't heard before. Perhaps she was simply homesick. But crafty foresight was his friend again. As was the case three years before at Liverpool, he had arranged a clause in his contract limiting his transfer fee to £500,000, the better to negotiate a hefty salary with his next club. We have already noted the weird machinations whereby Lawrie McMenemy at Southampton secured Keegan's signature. It was the second unlikely move of his career – as unlikely as Harry Kane one day returning from Bayern Munich to sign for Bournemouth – and prompts a question:

did Keegan prefer to avoid clubs where he wouldn't be the star player? Under Shankly's patronage he was swiftly elevated to 'inspiration of the team' and remained so for the next six years. Liverpool, in fact, had a first-option clause that meant he could return there, but with Kenny Dalglish now the darling of the Anfield crowd the prospect of playing second fiddle *and* in a different-numbered shirt held no attraction.

At Hamburg he had been guaranteed star billing, and so he would be at his next club. But instead of playing among the Ferraris of Italy he would be at the wheel of an Austin Maxi. A Masonic secrecy shrouded the move. He was almost certainly the first-ever Southampton recruit to arrive by private jet. At this point even Harry Swales, Keegan's agent, knew nothing of his client's next move. McMenemy had organised a press conference to unveil his 'mystery signing' at the Potters Heron Hotel, near Romsey; one can imagine the shock when he said to the assembled, 'I've got a bit of a surprise for you, lads,' and Keegan walked in. He explained that he had joined the Saints because he wanted another tilt at the First Division title, and why shouldn't he help bring it home to the Dell? It would make some story.

As ever with Keegan, pragmatism was a handmaid to romance. By now he was twenty-nine, in the form of his life and fitter than he had ever been. But the ruthless training methods of the Hamburger SV coach Branko Zebec were taking their toll on his body, and he'd begun to worry that if he stayed there, he might just burn out. The switch to Southampton offered a less brutal regime alongside the traditional competitiveness of the English game. Not much less brutal, it transpired. On Friday nights training would consist of vicious indoor five-a-side games in which players clobbered seven bells out of one another. Keegan at first complained to McMenemy that the sessions were no better than pub football, and risked injury to boot. The manager stood his ground: the players enjoyed this thuggery, and soon enough Keegan did, too. You might end up black and blue, but the team spirit it engendered was 'tremendous'. During his two seasons there Keegan's teammates were illustrious but ageing: Alan Ball, Mick Mills, Dave Watson, Mick Channon and Peter Shilton were all past thirty,* and even with the support base of younger talent a title challenge was going to be a stretch.

Still, McMenemy had pulled off a genuine coup and handed the captaincy to Keegan for the first game of

---

* Q: What did Keegan and these five Southampton players also have in common? A: They had all at one time captained England. Put that in your next football quiz.

the 1980–81 season, a 2–0 victory against Manchester City. 'Every ground we went to that season had their biggest crowd to see Kevin Keegan,' McMenemy later recalled. Southampton finished in sixth place, their best ever in the First Division, and everyone at the club was delighted.

Everyone but Keegan, that is. His expectations were different, and a sixth-place finish wasn't going to satisfy a recent two-time winner of the European Footballer of the Year award. He had seen enough to realise his own ambition far outstripped that of the club, and that investment wasn't uppermost in the board's mind. He was also unimpressed by McMenemy's approach to the care of his players. During a game against Birmingham, Keegan felt his hamstring go, and instead of taking him off McMenemy asked him to switch to the right wing and soldier on, thus exacerbating the injury. This foolishness was amplified later during a sponsors' trip to Morocco, where the ardour of the fans' worship surprised even Keegan. He was still *hors de combat*, but as the star turn he was obliged to make the journey, even if he couldn't play. Resting in the hotel, Keegan got a panicked call from McMenemy in the stadium, where the crowd were mightily miffed, chanting 'Kevin Keegan' and demanding to know where he was. If he didn't get there pronto, there'd be a riot. So the kick-off was delayed while a police escort rushed Keegan to the ground; ever the trouper, he got his leg strapped up and hobbled around for seventy minutes. A lesson in the downside of fame.

There were goals galore from him – 30 – in his second season, but the Southampton defence was too leaky to make that contribution count. They shipped 67 goals, especially galling for Keegan, who had urged McMenemy to sign Peter Shilton far earlier than he did. A bid for the title was derailed by a hopeless run of form and a late surge from Liverpool, who were still dogging his steps. Top of the table in April, Saints finished seventh, 21 points adrift. The thunderclouds over the Dell were all too visible. McMenemy may have been blind to his star's disgruntlement, for relations deteriorated drastically after a humiliating loss at home to Villa, when the manager bawled out the team as 'cheats'. Keegan took particular offence at the word, and despite having signed a new contract the previous November he told the club he was leaving at the end of the season. The fans were distraught, especially those who had bought season tickets on the understanding that Keegan would be at the Dell for another year.

I wonder if McMenemy's heated accusation was the catalyst, or if in fact Keegan had already made up his mind to leave. Pathologically restless, he relied on instinct as often as reason, and something was urging him to move on. Southampton had been an experiment, an attempt to haul an unfancied club to the top through his star wattage, leadership and will to win. For the first time in his career he discovered that not even his transformative potency could turn around a club that was content to stay small.

(*above*) Donny Boy: as a teenager in Doncaster.

(*above right*) Playing for Scunthorpe c.1969. Room for two of him in those shorts.

Earning his stripes. With his manager/mentor/surrogate father, Bill Shankly.

(*top*) Hear the roar: stepping out at Anfield in his
LFC debut, August 1971.

(*bottom*) Disbelief! Sent off against Leeds United in the
Charity Shield, August 1974.

(*top*) Get in. Scoring for England against Scotland at Wembley.

(*bottom*) Better than a Crispy Pancake. Delighting the Geordie crowd.

(*top*) In happier times, with headphones . . .

(*bottom*) Head Over Heels. Jean and Kevin in love
and long coats. Aww.

(*clockwise*) Say it with flowers – in his permtastic pomp.

On yer bike. *Superstars*, 1976, preparing to race.

Safety First. Reminding the nation how to cross the road ('keep your eyes open') in a 1976 public information campaign.

Brut and charisma. With sparring partner Henry Cooper.

(*top*) Cracking up with Emlyn Hughes outside Number 10.
Mrs T. not quite getting the joke.

(*bottom*) New Labour, Old Tricks. Head tennis with Tony,
Brighton, 1995.

(*top*) LOVE IT! The Keegan Rant, Elland Road, 29 April 1996.
One for the ages.

(*bottom*) Goodbye to all that. Walking through the rain at Wembley,
on his way to resigning as manager of England.

(*top*) Blue Moon: standing alone with the old First Division trophy that took Man City to the Premier League.

(*bottom*) Munich, 1973: chaired off the pitch after LFC win the UEFA Cup 3–2 on aggregate against Borussia Mönchengladbach.
It was his and the club's first European trophy.

5
THE VICTIM

I have observed that people who care little about football nevertheless know two things about Kevin Keegan. One is the perm. The other is the story of his being beaten up on a motorway lay-by. Why this should be is hard to construe, except that lurid details tend to have a long shelf life in the public imagination. In the case of this assault the circumstances and the identity of the victim were so outlandish as to lend it the air of an urban myth. How had a housewives' favourite, former captain of England and perm-haired trendsetter become embroiled in something that sounded like an episode of *Crimewatch*? And why did a rumour catch hold that the victim was implicated in a sex crime?

Strange to tell, but this wasn't the first time Keegan had been on the wrong end of grievous bodily harm. Back in 1974 he was just entering his imperial phase, scoring twice* as LFC beat Newcastle 3–0 in a one-

---

* His first goal prompted a line of commentary from the BBC's David Coleman ('Goals pay the rent, and Keegan does his share') that was feeble even by his low standards. Goals do not

sided FA Cup final and making the headlines later in the summer when he was sent off for brawling with Billy Bremner. In between these high/low points he found himself in a terrifying, almost Kafkaesque ordeal at Belgrade airport. England were on a tour of Eastern Europe under caretaker manager Joe Mercer, who was filling in after Alf Ramsey had been sacked. They had drawn 1–1 with East Germany in Leipzig and beaten Bulgaria 1–0 in Sofia. From there they flew to Yugoslavia. The FA's travel agent hadn't realised that Sofia was one hour ahead of Belgrade, and consequently no Yugoslav officials were there to greet the England party. Drinking onboard was a commonplace, and a Bulgarian stewardess complained that she'd been sexually harassed by one of the players. Keegan couldn't be arraigned on either count, since he'd been asleep the whole flight.

The team, in their civvies, must have looked a bedraggled bunch as they came through immigration. Perhaps to the authorities behind the Iron Curtain their rowdiness was a provocation. Keegan recalled laughing as Alec Lindsay, his Liverpool teammate, started fooling about on the luggage carousel. But

---

pay the rent, and exactly what 'share' of Keegan's was he on about – scoring or rent-paying?

the laughter died in his throat when he himself was grabbed from behind and dragged off to a back room. Once in there he was forced to kneel 'like a prisoner of war' as men in uniform began to punch, club and kick him. Appeals for mercy only incensed them further, and after twenty minutes Keegan, bleeding from his head and nose, became scared for his life. Fortunately, the FA's secretary, Ted Croker, arrived in time and explained to the police that Keegan wasn't a football hooligan but an England international; it says something about that benighted country that none of his assailants recognised him.

On being released he was examined by the team doctor. There was nothing broken, but the sight of him so appalled the other players that there was a move to cancel the game and catch the next flight home. Mercer managed to calm the mood and persuaded them to stay. He offered Keegan a chance to sit out the game, which was refused: on no account would he lose an England cap on top of everything else. He got a measure of revenge by scoring a late equaliser in the 2–2 draw. Shaken and humiliated by the assault, Keegan vowed never to return to Yugoslavia. When Hamburg drew Hajduk Split in a European Cup game years later he told his manager, Branko Zebec, he wouldn't be going. The latter, himself a Yugoslav, was horrified by the story of his bashing in the Balkans – it wasn't widely reported at the time – but eventually convinced Keegan that the incident was an aberration and that his countrymen in fact held him in high regard. The player eventually relented.

One upshot of the Belgrade beating was that henceforward blazers with a collar and tie would be mandatory wear for England football teams on tour. Three Lions on the breast pocket. Question: did this afford actual protection from police thugs or incite them to greater violence?

Cut to April 1991. Keegan had been living with the family in Marbella for seven years, playing a lot of golf, enjoying the weather and the anonymity and not thinking much at all about football. Following a serious discussion with Jean, they decided it was time to return to England. A number of factors were in play: their daughters' secondary education, his occasional commentary work for ITV and (inevitably) the tax year. Jean and the kids had flown home ahead, while Keegan chose to pack the Range Rover with their possessions and drive himself from Spain to the ferry at Calais. A 1,600-mile trip with only a brief overnight stop had left him underslept by the time he reached the ferry. A long chat with a Spurs fan onboard deprived him of a chance to take a nap, and once through customs he hit the motorway to Southampton, a couple of hours away.

Fatigue soon got the better of him. He jerked awake as a car in his rear mirror honked furiously: he must have been drifting out of his lane. Time to take a rest. He pulled off the M25 at Reigate and sought a lay-by where he could park and put his head down. The noise of whizzing traffic forced him to go further off-road, and he eventually found 'a dark lane', where he stopped the car, propped a pillow against the window and quickly fell asleep.

He would be thankful for that pillow, because at some point – maybe an hour or more after he'd parked – a rock smashed against his car window, swiftly followed by a man setting about him with a baseball bat. But for the pillow's protection he might already have been dead; as it was, he now had a bat thrust in his face and unknown assailants yelling for his wallet. Cash and credit cards were surrendered, and as suddenly as they arrived his tormentors were gone. Dazed and terrified, Keegan tried to start the car, only to find his tyres had been slashed and the luggage taken. He staggered out to the main road and managed to flag down a passing motorist, who called for the police and an ambulance.

I have sometimes thought of that Good Samaritan, and wonder at the courage it took for him (or her) to go to his aid. There you are, tootling along a dark country road, minding your own business, when all of a sudden a gashed and bloodied figure looms out in front of you like Banquo's ghost. Some impulse of pity or compassion forces you to pull over, get out of your car and approach the man, smallish, hysterical, vaguely familiar and hurrying through his story in Spanish (in his groggy state he'd forgotten he was back in England). How long is it before comprehension dawns and you realise that this battered and traumatised person is *Kevin Keegan*?*

At the hospital a doctor put eight stitches in his scalp. Despite the baseball bat to the mouth, Keegan still had all his teeth. He was bloody, bruised, but intact. For all his injuries, he knew that he'd been lucky to walk away. As Cormac McCarthy once said, 'You never know what worse luck your bad luck has

---

* The more I think about this scene, the more it strikes me as a great opening to a screenplay – not about Kevin Keegan, but about someone driving home down a lonely road at night and encountering the victim of a savage mugging, whom he helps to safety. That the victim is a celebrity, and his saviour is initially unaware of his fame, already shimmers with dramatic potential. Imagine what Hitchcock might have done with the scenario.

saved you from.' All the same, it would have taken Keegan – anyone – some time to process this misfortune in philosophical terms. Anger and bewilderment would be roiling in the blood. 'Why me?' is the instinctive response to such an episode, and it would toll in the head for many days and nights afterwards. As the police began to apprehend Keegan's attackers, the story emerged of a drug gang in debt to a supplier. In need of quick cash, they had spotted a Range Rover parked off the motorway and with ruthless opportunism decided to rob its sleeping owner. They had no idea of his identity until they were rifling through the contents of his wallet hours later. Their celebrity victim would make for a good story, and in fact it was one of the gang bragging about it in a Newhaven pub that gave them away.

In the aftermath, Keegan went back and forth to Reigate police station, identifying items of his stolen property and trying to piece together what had happened. On a later visit he was told that the suspects were being held in a cell on the premises. In his autobiography Keegan candidly recalls asking one of the CID officers to give him a baseball bat so he could 'give them a taste of their own medicine'. The officer was 'very understanding' but turned down his request, explaining to him that nowadays criminals tended to have more rights than their victims. Keegan as Old Testament avenger had to go back in his box.

In the event, three of the gang were tried in court and given prison sentences. But the matter didn't rest there. It so happened that Keegan had parked at a spot notorious in that part of Surrey as a lovers' rendez-vous, or, to adopt a term not then in popular use, a dogging site. The youthfulness of his assailants – the baseball-bat wielder was in his teens – inflamed the gossip surrounding the case. The tabloids dispatched their dirt-diggers and soon scurrilous tales of underage sex and blackmail were springing from the mulch like poison mushrooms. That none of these stories ever held up validates Keegan's innocence, but lack of evidence doesn't stop the rumour mill grinding. Painful and humiliating enough for him to have been assaulted in the first place. Far more galling to watch the episode take on an afterlife of baseless conspiracy theories and tap-of-the-nose insinuation. Today they call it 'reputational damage', though Shakespeare expressed the true hurt four hundred years earlier:

> Who steals my purse steals trash; 'tis something, nothing;
> 'Twas mine, 'tis his, and has been slave to thousands:

But he that filches from me my good name
Robs me of that which not enriches him
And makes me poor indeed.*

Keegan would understand that, although I don't imagine him being so nonchalant about someone stealing his purse.

---

* *Othello*, Act III, Scene iii.

6
THE SECOND COMING

Q: Which famous 'son of Newcastle' speaks without a trace of a Geordie accent? Is it (a) Kevin Keegan or (b) Michael Caine as Jack Carter in the 1971 film *Get Carter*? The answer, of course, is both, though I accept that at least one of them is a fictional character. In the last twenty years the film has gone from cult favourite to seminal Brit *noir*, and yet rare are the objections to Caine's Bermondsey twang. Accents matter, especially in a crime drama that prides itself on gritty realism. 'Place' can have as much character in a story as people, and the suspension of disbelief we grant to storytellers can end up hanged by the neck if they don't get the details right.

Jack Carter made his first appearance in Ted Lewis's 1970 novel *Jack's Return Home*. Having abandoned his native Newcastle for London and the criminal life, Jack takes no pleasure in his homecoming. It hasn't changed at all in the eight years he's been away – 'A good place to say goodbye to.' It's a sombre mission that's brought him back: to discover the truth of his brother Frank's

mysterious death. The novel was a bestseller on its pub-
lication and gained greater traction when it was filmed
the following year as *Get Carter* by Mike Hodges. The
Newcastle setting allowed the film-makers a dramatic
visual contrast between the back-to-back terraces of
the old mining community and the grim concrete and
asphalt high-rises that post-war urban planners had
been dreaming up to replace them.*

Down these mean cobbled streets a man must go,
who is himself mean. Michael Caine looks great in
the title role, tall and imposing, and the trench coat
he wears fairly bristles with intent. When Bogart wore
one it was a signifier of moral goodness – first as Rick
in *Casablanca*, then as Marlowe in *The Big Sleep* – only
his was a light colour. Carter's trench coat is black,
foreshadowing the diabolical mayhem he's about to
unleash.† His narrow eyes and slot mouth turn out to
be those of a pitiless killer. Everything in the performance is finely judged – except for the accent. Granted,
he's been away from his home town for years, yet
still there would be – should be – singsong notes of

* Most infamously, the Gateshead multi-storey car park, from
whose heights Carter hurls businessman Cliff Brumby to his
doom. The building's iconic notoriety didn't save it from the
wrecking ball in 2010.
† Or maybe he's Death himself, like Dylan's 'Man in the Long
Black Coat'.

Geordie in the voice. But Caine was no student of accents – listen to his mangling of American in *The Cider House Rules* (for which he won an inexplicable Oscar). Jack Carter speaks in uninflected cockney, and nobody finds it strange or even noteworthy.

Fast-forward twenty years, and Newcastle were preparing to welcome home another exile. Keegan hadn't thought about football very much while he was in Spain. He had also made it clear that he would never be a manager. It seemed he had found contentment enough in Hampshire with his family and his horses. In the seven years since he'd been there as a player Newcastle United had become another bin fire, selling off their best players and discarding managers in a cycle that was now all bust and no boom. Peter Beardsley had gone to Liverpool for £1.9 million in 1987. Paul Gascoigne, their most gifted player in a generation, went to Spurs for £2.2 million a year later. Instead of being among the clubs involved in setting up the new Premier League, Newcastle were once more in the Second Division, and not doing so well there. An internecine war was tearing the board apart, a share issue had flopped and the club was up to its waist in debt.

The arrival of John Hall to bale it out came in the nick of time. He cleared out the board's old guard and, in what amounted to a coup, installed his son, Douglas, along with certain trusted lieutenants. With classic timing, the directors had just given the current manager, Ossie Ardiles, a public vote of confidence; privately, there were already moves afoot to sack him.

So who would take charge of the team? Someone who 'bled black and white', obviously. Someone whose passion would excite the fans again, undoubtedly. Someone who could save them from dropping into the Third Division, urgently. There could only be one candidate. At some point the call would have gone out: *Get Keegan.* Perhaps followed by, 'Shall we send the helicopter again?'

And he wasn't even a Geordie.*

---

* But he did have a northern accent and sensibility, unlike Caine's Jack Carter. I sometimes wonder if Caine and Keegan ever met. It's not unlikely, perhaps at some black-tie charity event in the 1970s or early '80s. The country's most famous footballer and its most famous actor must have crossed paths, greeted one another with the mechanical bonhomie that all celebrities adopt on first meeting, like a Masonic handshake. The actor towering over the footballer, the whiff of Caine's cigar against the great smell of Brut. Perhaps Keegan had seen *Get Carter* and jokingly asked Caine how he'd got away with being a cockney geezer with roots in Newcastle. Caine, with no ear for accents, wouldn't have noticed that Keegan wasn't a Geordie himself. Come to think of it, Keegan would have made good casting in the 1981 POW movie *Escape to Victory*, in which Caine plays (don't laugh) a former pro footballer in charge of the prison team due to play the Reich's finest in occupied Paris. Bobby Moore, Pelé and Sylvester Stallone also feature,

*

'There's never a better time to take over a club than when it's down,' Keegan said later, but even he seemed to realise he'd been impulsive in accepting Hall's offer. In February 1992 Newcastle were second from bottom in the league, with 16 games to go. He had almost no clue about the players he would be relying upon, or about their future opponents, or about the Second Division in general. The job always carried a risk, but this time the challenge felt scary. He didn't want to be remembered as (dread phrase) *the manager who took the club down* ... What if he put the mess into 'messiah'? Hall had offered him £60,000 from February to May, with a bonus of £60,000 if he kept them up. The deal was signed and a press conference held. He almost dropped a clanger with his first words: 'I can honestly say there's no job in football I've ever wanted.' Eh? Then he hurriedly added, 'This is the only job I've ever wanted.' Phew – saved himself.

As ever, the force of his self-belief overcame any misgivings. He didn't know what it was to fail, and his experience of playing at the highest level would armour

----

as does about half of the Ipswich Town squad, filling in for the match sequences. 'You've never seen anything like it,' the trailer announces. Was Keegan not available? Or could the production not afford him?

him for the fight ahead. He had spent years among great football men – Shankly, Paisley, Alf Ramsey, Don Revie, Joe Mercer. 'I would have been a fool not to have learned from these people,' he reflected. But Keegan had learned from them only as a player. He had no grounding at all as a manager or a coach, no grasp of the day-to-day responsibilities. Even if he'd had the training, it was arguable whether he had the temperament. Yes, Shankly was ebullient and mercurial, too, but not only that. He was tactically clued-up, he understood mind games, he inspired fear, he could be ruthless when the moment required. Keegan wasn't any of that, and he never learned to be.

His first hire as a manager would not have inspired confidence. His old pal Terry McDermott had also been out of the game for years and now made a living selling hamburgers at racecourses. One can picture his surprise when Keegan called, asking him to be his right-hand man at St James's Park. Friends reunited. That beat flipping burgers! Anticipating queries from the board, Keegan arranged to pay him out of his own pocket until the end of the season. He called McDermott his 'buffer', though given how little either of them knew about the current Newcastle set-up it might as well have been 'bluffer'. The realisation of how low their old club had fallen came on transfer deadline day, March 1992. With hopes of clearing out a few players to streamline the squad and cut down the wage bill, the two of them waited by the phone, ready to strike deals. The 5 p.m. deadline passed, and the phone had stayed silent. Not a single enquiry. Nobody wanted a player from Newcastle.

Worse was to follow, and it almost provoked Keegan to walk out on the club, 37 days after he'd arrived. He had already organised a clean-up of the club's facilities – the state of disrepair had shocked him – and made sure that the players no longer had to wash their own kit. What disturbed him more were the ongoing shenanigans in the boardroom, where John Hall had been cooking up a contract that reneged on the money he'd promised for transfers. When Keegan got wind of it he was furious, and not for the first time in his career he stormed off. McDermott calmed him, temporarily, arguing that they shouldn't leave the team in the lurch. So the pair of them went back to Newcastle, oversaw the game against Swindon on the Saturday (they won 3–1) and parted – seemingly for good – with a handshake and no hard feelings.

Back in Hampshire Keegan brooded, waiting for a telephone call from his employer. This was no bluff. 'Sir John Hall could not expect Kevin Keegan to manage Newcastle on empty promises, especially when 36,000 fans believed in me.' Note the reference to himself in the third person, something that is quite frequent in his 1997 autobiography. Even allowing for the ghost-writer gussying up the drama, Keegan is the kind of man who likes to project himself rhetorically, emphatically. He doesn't mean to, but it can come across as pompous and blustering. A good friend might have advised him not to keep referring to himself as 'Kevin Keegan', and perhaps he listened. Between the second and third autobiographies the habit thins out, and the story reads better for it.

Hall did ring, and cleared the air. He assured Keegan that only two people could save the club: namely, the two talking on the phone together at that moment. The new manager would get the money for transfers, the chairman promised, and from that day they were as close as a pair of magpies.

Meanwhile, the new manager 'bounce' was working, with only two losses in the first nine games. Keegan recalls McDermott predicting that they could go from now till the end of the season unbeaten, whereupon their form dropped off a cliff. They lost the next five in a row, including a 6–2 spanking at Wolves. Part of the problem was that the new management still weren't sure which were their best players, or indeed *who* were their players. One day a young lad walked in whom

Keegan had never seen before. It transpired his name was Billy Askew and he had been on loan to a Third Division club. But no one had bothered telling the boss. He rated certain players – Gavin Peacock, David Kelly, Brian Kilcline – but some of the older professionals seemed indifferent and disconnected from the club. To someone of Keegan's do-or-die commitment it was infuriating.

With two games left to play Newcastle were in the bottom three and staring down the barrel of relegation. The first they won with a late David Kelly goal against Portsmouth. It went down to the wire, away to Leicester – 'gut-wrenching', as Keegan recalls it. With the score at 1–1 a Steve Walsh own goal handed Keegan's team a last-minute victory. The crowd, unsurprisingly, were on the pitch. The club was safe, for now. He had patched up the listing vessel and somehow stopped it from going down.

But how to make an ocean liner out of this shipwreck? Keegan started by straightening things out with Hall and the directors. He had been presented with another contract that meant he would have to sell players to buy new ones. Groundhog Day. Once again, he left town in disgust, this time disappearing to his home in Spain. A delegation led by Douglas Hall flew out to negotiate a new deal; they assured him that

Newcastle were going to match his ambitions, and that he was the man to take them into the Premier League. *Come home, Kev*. Keegan agreed to a three-year contract, with Terry McDermott confirmed as his assistant manager.

Now the caulking and refitting and streamlining could properly begin. Keegan's recruitment that season of 1992–93 was spot on. He signed below-the-radar talents – John Beresford, Paul Bracewell and Barry Venison – to shore up the defence, and later brought in key players such as Rob Lee and Scott Sellars. His most significant piece of business almost didn't happen. One evening he and McDermott took a quixotic ride south on Douglas Hall's private jet. Their destination was Ashton Gate to watch Bristol City play West Ham, in order to get a proper look at the home side's free-scoring centre-forward, Andy Cole.

Cole, his thigh strapped up that evening, was evidently carrying an injury. His greyhound turn of pace was compromised, and he had to be subbed early. McDermott considered the trip a waste of time. Keegan thought otherwise: Cole impressed him for playing despite his injury. Wasn't this just the type of spirit he wanted to replicate at Newcastle? He was keener than ever to sign him, although his initial overtures went awry. In his first phone call to the player

Keegan mistakenly addressed him as 'Anthony Cole'. Pushing past the embarrassment he told the player that Newcastle were prepared to break their transfer record to sign him, and hoped he would get on a flight from Heathrow that evening. With every show of coolness Cole replied that he had something else on that night, so a meeting would have to wait. (Keegan later discovered that Cole's previous engagement was in fact his laundry night – he had no clean clothes to wear.)

Having got Cole to Newcastle – and thus delighted every pun-minded football headline writer in the land – Keegan's hunch proved sound. Playing the last 12 games of the 1992–93 season Cole notched 12 goals, helping to catapult the team into the Premier League in style. Their haul of 96 points was eight ahead of West Ham, with 92 goals and an average home gate of just over 29,000. Even the defence, Keegan's smallest zone of interest, had conceded only 38 goals – the best defensive record in the division, after having the worst (84) the previous season.

Confidence was high as the club entered its honeymoon season in the Premier League, and after a double hiccup of defeats – home to Spurs and away to Coventry – they put their first points on the board with a 1–1 draw at Old Trafford, Cole scoring the equaliser. He continued in that vein, scoring 34 goals in 40 games, including a hat-trick in a 3–0 home win against Liverpool. He scored again in their 2–0 victory at Anfield, completing a rare double in the fixture. He wasn't the first player to thrive on the hard, selfless work of his strike partner, Peter Beardsley, another signing in pre-season. A veteran now at thirty-two, he also scored 25 goals of his own.*

Keegan could feel proud of the club's third-place finish that season, which had earned them a spot in Europe. But with success comes heightened expectations. The ardour from the home terraces was pressure enough; now the pundits were talking of Newcastle's title challenge. 'Coming third is very different from coming first,' as Keegan soberly noted. A title bid would pose a dilemma. Should the team continue in their open, swashbuckling style – the Cavaliers to Man Utd's Roundheads – or should they adopt a more pragmatic approach and learn how to close games out? Keegan believed it his responsibility to give the fans what they wanted, which in a nutshell was 'pure entertainment'. If the opposition scored three, then they would score four. If it was a choice between buying a flair player or one who could 'do a job', he would go

---

* Gary Lineker reckons Beardsley was the best player he was ever partnered with.

for flair. In retrospect he saw that this was a hostage to fortune. A more measured approach, and a better appreciation of the dreary basics ('do a job'), could have sprung him from the trap he had laid for himself.

In the documentary *Keegan on Keegan* there's a revealing passage where he gives a brief history of managerial disappointments at Newcastle:

> Every time a manager took over here I thought, 'He's gonna do it.' Arthur Cox'll do it for sure . . . all right, something happened, he went. Jack Charlton, tremendous choice, he'll do it. Didn't last long. Willy McFaul, local lad, yeah, he's got the passion, he'll do it . . . Didn't make it. Jim Smith, yeah, must do it, knew him from Boston. He'll do the work and the club will grow under him. Didn't happen. Then Ossie Ardiles, I thought, yeah, masterstroke, he's gotta be the one, the club'll play good football, the fans will love him, they're sure to get out if they get the right players. Didn't happen. Now it's my turn . . . I just hope it happens.

Two things to note: how like a fan he sounds; and how (alas) like David Brent, with his pile-up of names ('after Slough there's Reading, Aldershot,

Bracknell . . .') and the deflating, inadvertent comedy of repetition ('didn't last long . . . didn't happen . . . didn't happen'). Then the bathetic finale of 'I just hope it happens'.

The mood at St James's Park remained upbeat. Keegan had bought the Belgian Philippe Albert to join Darren Peacock in the centre of defence, and he saw the team get off to a flyer, winning their first six games of the 1994–95 season. They continued unbeaten until the end of October, when they lost 2–0 at Old Trafford. One of United's scorers that day was a young winger, Keith Gillespie, who would play a significant part in the biggest story of Newcastle's season. In January 1995 Keegan, seeking to bolster the squad, rang Alex Ferguson to enquire about Gillespie's availability. United were in the middle of an overhaul and needed a new striker; perhaps scenting a coup, Ferguson let it be known Keegan could have Gillespie as part of an exchange with Andy Cole. To his surprise – and everybody else's – Keegan agreed. A £6 million fee, plus Gillespie, constituted the deal.

What had happened? Cole had played 84 games for Newcastle and scored 68 goals, an astonishing return. He was the toast of the Tyne and probably the best centre-forward in the country. His transfer at this point would hand United a huge advantage in their run at the title. Keegan understood this, and yet he was still prepared to sell. He reasoned that Cole was no longer fully committed to the club, had begun to 'skive' in training and his goals had dried up. In short, they had got the best out of the player, and with that much money on the table it would be wiser to move him on.* The board had to back the manager's decision. But how would the fans react?

When the news broke it stunned the city. Fans began to head for the ground, and soon a crowd was forming outside. TV crews followed. Shock had curdled into anger, and Douglas Hall, fearing the worst, asked security to bring two getaway cars round to the other side of the stadium. But instead of scarpering, Keegan did what no other manager would have contemplated: he went onto the steps of the Milburn Stand and faced the mob. It was a theatrical gesture, like Mark Antony declaiming on the steps of the Senate after Caesar's assassination. Keegan, his laurels (and possibly his life) under threat, gave ear to the outrage. Why was he letting go of his best player? Had Newcastle reverted to type and become a selling club? Cries of 'Judas' and 'traitor' split the air. After more heckling the crowd

---

* In his 2018 autobiography Keegan suggests Cole had been 'tapped up', though he has no evidence and believes no one at Old Trafford would ever admit to it.

began to listen. Keegan owned it as his decision, and he would take the blame if it turned out wrong. He explained that the money from Cole would go back into the team; that they had a good signing in Keith Gillespie; that he had not let them down so far. The mood softened as fans realised how unusual it was for a manager to talk to them directly.

Inevitably, another concern was raised. With Andy Cole gone, where would the goals come from? As Keegan tells it, a fan came eloquently to his rescue: the manager wouldn't dream of selling Cole without having a replacement lined up, now would he? Keegan must have suppressed a blush, for of course he *didn't* have a replacement lined up. But the fans weren't to know that. By the time he waved them goodbye (exit stage left) they looked warily mollified. Keegan, the bridge-burner, the instinct artist, had won a reprieve.

7
THE CONTENDER

The story of the 1995–96 Premier League season belongs unquestionably to Kevin Keegan, albeit not for the reason he would have liked. The Newcastle campaign has become English football's *locus classicus* of The Nearly Men, or The One That Got Away. Whenever the story is told, other than by the red half of Manchester, it is usually in tones of sighing, head-shaking regret. In racing terms the team did a Devon Loch, the Queen's horse that collapsed 40 yards from the winning post at the 1956 Grand National. Yet Devon Loch's name is now enshrined in sporting legend, and who remembers the name of the winning horse that day?

Keegan's personal popularity was undiminished. When Labour held its party conference at Brighton in October 1995 Tony Blair almost fell over himself to get an audience with Keegan, who had come to town for a fringe meeting. There is famous footage of the two, both in white shirts, playing head tennis with a football. 'At last,' said Blair, 'I have done something to impress my children.' Aged forty-two, Blair was then the coming man, preparing the ground for the general election two years ahead. Maybe he thought he could learn something from Keegan's gathering momentum as the People's Favourite.

That in the autumn of 1995 his Newcastle side were being hailed as 'the entertainers' and 'the neutrals' favourite' would have been music to Keegan's ears. The team were carrying all before them, and with a swagger that almost defied belief: this was the club that had fought off relegation from the Second Division only three years before. He had kept his word about using the Cole money and in the summer had bought David Ginola, Les Ferdinand and Warren Barton, at that time the most expensive defender (£4 million) in English football. In August they hit the ground running with four straight wins and by Christmas were top of the league: P19, W14, D3, L2. Midfielder Rob Lee recalls Keegan nutshelling his management philosophy: 'I buy good players and let them play.' Tactics were for others. They barely changed formation, unless there were injuries. His basic instruction was for Ginola and Gillespie to supply crosses to Les Ferdinand, 'the best header of the ball in the country'. By the halfway point of the season Ferdinand had already bagged 18 goals.

Their lead over Manchester Utd was ten points when they met on 27 December at Old Trafford. Ferguson was perhaps still smarting from Alan Hansen's impertinent 'you can't win anything with kids' remark on *Match of the Day* following their 3–1 defeat to Villa on the opening day. But second in the league wasn't bad. Hansen's theory didn't hold water in any case: alongside the 'kids' Ferguson could also rely on proven title-winners like Schmeichel, Keane, Bruce, Irwin and Pallister. His talisman, Cantona, was back following the nine-month ban for kung-fu fighting at Selhurst Park. In the event United won 2–0, their first goal scored – oh, irony! – by Andy Cole.

United had cut the gap to seven points, and then squandered the advantage by losing 4–1 to Spurs and drawing 0–0 at home to Villa. The following week Newcastle beat Coventry 1–0 to go 12 points clear. That oft-quoted '12-point lead' in fact lasted only a few days; the vagaries of the fixture list meant that Newcastle had a game in hand for much of this period, and United were closer on their tail than is commonly believed. Know-how in title chases was a key difference between them. Ferguson, a wily campaigner, understood pressure and the vulnerabilities that attended it. I still recall the hope and dread I felt for Keegan and his team, waveringly on top and leaping from one game to the next like scaffolders on heights. It looked vertiginous up there.

Luck played its part as the season wore on. Gillespie had suffered an abdominal injury in the Old Trafford game and his absence disrupted the team's shape. Keegan moved Beardsley to the right, and then decided – fatefully, as some believed – to dip into the transfer market. He bought David Batty from Blackburn, as a shield for the defence, and Colombian Tino Asprilla, a brilliant and capricious winger Keegan believed could revitalise his attack.* That was borne out in his first game, when he came off the bench against Middlesbrough and turned a 1–0 deficit on its head with two assists. Two weeks later the player's volatile temperament made the headlines when he nutted Manchester City's Keith Curle. The press had conniptions, Newcastle were held to a 3–3 draw, and a belief took hold that Asprilla was bad luck.

---

* Asprilla's arrival in Newcastle was unforgettable, all smiles and wrapped up in a long fur coat amid a Tyneside snowstorm – or was it on a tailwind of Colombian blow? Tino was a gift to the newspapers. He already had a court order against him after firing a handgun during a celebration on New Year's Day, and had to report to the Colombian embassy in London every week. Keegan had no regrets about signing him, and claimed without irony that the firearm incident was 'blown up out of all proportion'.

It calls to mind a similar story from the title run-in of 1971–72, when Malcolm Allison's Manchester City bagged Rodney Marsh in a statement signing from QPR. At the time City were four points clear at the top, but suffered a dramatic deflation that allowed Brian Clough's Derby County to clinch the title by a point. City finished fourth. I'm not sure if Allison or Keegan felt buyer's remorse. While a single player's form can make the difference in winning a title, as Cantona's did in 1995–96, it seems implausible that a single player can *lose* you one* . . . unless, perhaps, it's a goalkeeper. And who would sign a keeper during a title run-in?

Next up was the crunch, a Monday game at home to United, with the momentum now hanging in the balance. In the first 20 minutes Newcastle nearly overwhelmed United, with Ferdinand twice denied by Schmeichel, whose performance that night was superhuman. 'I've never seen goalkeeping like that,' said Rob Lee in retrospect. 'He singlehandedly kept us out.'

At half-time no one could quite understand how it was goalless. Ferguson gave his team a rocket, berating

* And yet Marsh in his autobiography owned the blame precisely: 'I have to hold my hands up – I cost Manchester City the 1972 League Championship.'

his defenders for failing to pick up Asprilla. There's a hilarious clip of Gary Neville kicking fresh air like a can-can dancer. 'Play like that second half and you've cost us the title,' Ferguson told him. They came out looking far more composed, and determined. Cole, almost foreordained to be Keegan's nemesis, had a hand in the build-up to Cantona's goal in the 51st minute – the winner, as it transpired.

If that was hard to take, what happened four weeks later suggested that the Fates had it in for him. Anfield, 3 April 1996, was Keegan's Waterloo. An open game played at a febrile tempo, it has gone down as one for the ages in the Premier League's hall of fame. Twice Newcastle led, 2–1, then 3–2 (the third a magnificent outside-of-the-boot finish from Asprilla), until Liverpool clawed themselves back to parity midway through the second half. Then Stan Collymore broke Magpie hearts with a stoppage-time stunner. The sight of Keegan slumped over the advertising hoardings at the end was – even to my Liverpudlian eyes – piteous. I could have cried for him.

The wheels were coming off, but why? Keegan later said that the whole team suffered a critical loss of form and confidence. Being a heart-on-the-sleeve character he was probably not the sort of leader who could shield his own dismay for the sake of the collective good. The players would have noticed his brooding, his frustration, and realised that this long, wild ride was close to collapse. The ominous build-up of stress came to a head one evening at Elland Road. A few weeks earlier Man Utd had narrowly beaten struggling Leeds. Ferguson, with sly insinuation, said he hoped that Leeds would put in the same effort when Newcastle played them. He also noted that Newcastle had agreed to play a testimonial game on behalf of Stuart Pearce soon after the penultimate league fixture at the City Ground, the implication being that Forest would go easy on them as a mark of gratitude.

In the event Newcastle beat Leeds 1–0, but the memorable part of the occasion came afterwards in the tunnel at Elland Road. Interviewed from the Sky studio by Richard Keys and Andy Gray, Keegan looked underslept, and his brow was thunderous. He also sported a pair of outsize headphones, which may have deceived him as to his volume level.

> KEEGAN: I think things have to be said . . . I think you've got to send Alex Ferguson a tape of this game, haven't you? Isn't that what he asked for?
>
> GRAY: Well, I'm sure if he was watching it tonight, Kevin, he could have no arguments

about the way Leeds went about their job and
really tested your team.

KEEGAN: And . . . we're . . . we're playing Notts
Forest on Thursday, and he objected to that.
Now that was fixed up four months ago. We
were supposed to play Notts Forest. I mean,
that sort of stuff, we . . . It's been . . . We're
bet— we're bigger than that.

KEYS: But that's part and parcel of the
psychological battle of the game, Kevin, isn't
it?

KEEGAN: *No!* When you do that with footballers,
like he said about Leeds, and when you
do things like that about a man like Stuart
Pearce . . . I'm, I've kept really quiet. But
I'll tell you something: he went down in my
estimation when he said that. We have not
resorted to that. But I'll tell you – you can
tell him now, he'll be watching it – we're still
fighting for this title, and he's got to go to
Middlesbrough and get something, and . . . and
I'll tell you honestly, I will love it if we beat
them – *love it!*

The jabbing of his finger, the hoarseness of his
voice – you could almost hear Alex Ferguson tittering

over in Manchester. The Keegan Rant is another one for the ages, football's equivalent of Peter Finch throwing a wobbly in *Network* ('I'm mad as hell and I'm not going to take this any more!'). It's his proclamation of integrity, and something more.* When Keys refers to the 'psychological battle' intrinsic to the game, the vehemence of Keegan's reaction is revealing. He appears to regard Ferguson's attempt to psych him out as not only unfair but outrageous, insupportable – *dishonest*. 'We have not resorted to that,' he says, but 'that' is merely the age-old game of bluff, often known as 'kidology'. Keegan already knew the trick from his beloved mentor at Anfield. He likes to tell the story of himself as a young Liverpool player about to face Bobby Moore of West Ham, at that time the best defender in England.† Shankly tipped him the wink

---

* I should confess here that my obsession with this rant has been long and possibly unhealthy. I have watched it so often on YouTube that I know every intonation of it by heart. Some can recite Henry V before Agincourt, or Lincoln at Gettysburg, but my go-to set piece is Keegan at Elland Road. Writers spend a lot of time on their own, and in the dream-spaces between writing and worrying I hear myself quoting aloud bits of poems or lines from films . . . but also phrases such as 'love it!' and 'We have not resorted to that.' My wife is a long-suffering witness, and if she happens to be reading this, I hope she'll take it as my apology for the hours, the days, the years of what might be called repetitive Keeganitis.

† It is somehow typical of Keegan that he recalls his first encounter with Moore as coming at a toy fair in Brighton

that he'd just come from the visitors' dressing room and had found Moore looking 'scared stiff', hungover and limping. It was 'the Shanks psychology', Keegan recalled, a performative boost designed to pump up his protégé.

Which it duly did. Keegan had a good game, but afterwards Shankly admitted that Moore was actually a great player; he didn't want his lad thinking he'd just got the better of an inferior opponent. Kidology. Yet I don't recall Keegan being indignant on hearing 'things like that about a man like Bobby Moore'. Or that Shankly 'went down in my estimation when he said that'. I don't think it's hypocrisy on Keegan's part that he praises one manager and deplores another for the same practice. It is simply his naivety.

Newcastle lost the title, and the inquest made much of that epochal defeat at Anfield. But in truth it was their form in February and March that had holed them below the waterline. Even after Anfield they might have rallied. They were 1–0 up away to Blackburn

---

while promoting 'a plastic football made by Mettoy'. As well as being a World Cup-winning captain and one of the all-time great defenders, Moore ran various commercial ventures, and he gave the young Keegan 'useful advice' on his outside interests. Not that useful: the older man, unlike Keegan, mostly failed in business.

with minutes to go before being mugged 2–1. Then the 1–1 draws in their final two games against Forest and Spurs put the kibosh on their dimming hopes. United went to Middlesbrough on the last day and cleaned up, 3–0. Another manager, aping Ferguson's gamesmanship, might have suggested that Middlesbrough would have put up more of a fight had someone other than Bryan Robson – former United legend – been in their dugout. But that wasn't Keegan's style: he would not cast aspersions on his old England teammate, however tempted he might have been.

The reverberations proved more lasting for some than others. In his essayistic memoir *The North Will Rise Again* (2023) Alex Niven candidly admits he has never quite recovered from Keegan's 'heroic failure' of 1996. 'In common with many people from the North-East, I seem to have internalized the fairytale of Keegan's Newcastle over the years, so that few things I have experienced in the intervening years have come close to emulating this utopic digression of the mid-Nineties. This is the full, real, absurd and tragic implication of what it means to believe in the possibility of a messiah.' Niven identifies this belief as both comforting and stupefying, since it keeps alive the flame of romantic myth and at the same time reconciles the believer to accepting things cannot change without a semi-divine intervention. *Will ye no' come back again?* He calls this messianic fervour a 'vast melancholic illusion', particularly strong among the northern English. Bereft of faith in political leaders, or in the dinosaurs of the monarchy and the church, many in the North find their meaning in football – the club, the *esprit de corps*, the manager. As Keegan was to Newcastle, so Jürgen Klopp has been to Liverpool, turning 'doubters into believers'.

Maybe it's easy for a Liverpool fan to say, but I can't think of Keegan's Newcastle adventure as anything but glorious. That seat-of-the-pants assault on the league summit, the goals, the performances, the stumble, the rant: all wonderful. It's almost as good as football gets. I condole with Niven and understand his messiah theory. But I would no more count that season a failure than I would Liverpool's 2018–19 campaign, when they were pipped to the title by a single point, 98 to 97, on the last matchday.* Yes, a sickener for sure, and you can pick over all the moments when it might have been different. But it's only a failure if you regard winning as the be-all and end-all. It wasn't long after the disappointment of 2019 that I came back

---

* Or the 2021–22 season, come to that, when City beat us to the title, again by a single point.

to feeling grateful for the ride, and for having such a manager as Klopp. The memories are enough; they are much more than enough.

I wonder if Keegan has come round to that way of thinking.

8
THE DEAL-MAKER

He often seemed to be leaving places, or threatening to leave. His restlessness was incurable, and his impulsiveness made him reach for the door. After the emotional Vesuvius of 1995–96 he felt wiped out, and empty. The post-mortem on how he'd 'blown' the club's title bid dragged on. 'A part of me wondered if it was time to leave Newcastle.' For people of a certain character, confronting the possibility that you might leave is tantamount to accepting you're already gone. Keegan was one of them. The prospect of another season, another go-round with Ferguson and United, felt oppressive to him. He needed a rest, and told the Newcastle board it might be better if he stood down.

How seriously they took him is uncertain. He had threatened to quit before and pulled back. Perhaps this was his dry run for the proper resignation. But in July 1996 another event temporarily eclipsed his doubts. Alan Shearer had told Blackburn he wanted a move, and now the top two in the Premier League were desperate to sign him. Aware that the player had already spoken to Ferguson, Keegan probably felt that once again his rival was going to best him. Shearer had led the England line with honour at Euro 96 and his popularity was high; in a choice between proven champions and boyhood club the balance surely tipped towards the former. But by meeting Keegan – a hero of his youth – he was clearly setting his sights on St James's Park. The only request he made of the manager was that he wear the number 9 on his shirt. I imagine Keegan would have agreed to laser-print it on personally.

But still the deal hangs in the balance. Newcastle believe they have their man for £15 million – a world-record transfer at the time – until Blackburn owner Jack Walker gets back to Douglas Hall with a stipulation. He wants the cash in one lump sum rather than the usual payment by instalments. It's a staggering demand. Keegan, on hearing it, seems to be watching his dream player disappear in a vapour trail of zeroes . . . The good news is that Walker's demand to Man Utd is even steeper, £20 million, on account of a grudge from a previous deal. So the player will go to Newcastle, as long as they can stump up the money. Hall gets on the phone to his father, Sir John, who once again digs into his pocket and saves the day. The local hero is coming home.

'We have signed Alan Shearer,' Keegan announced in Bangkok, where the club was playing in a pre-season tournament, 'and we're delighted, obviously.' The following week, back at St James's Park, the coronation was held in front of thousands of fans. At the press conference, Keegan, in a wild floral tie (a duty-free purchase at the airport?), was in statesman-like mood: 'We've sold 'em off time and time again up here, and tried to replace them with other players very quickly. That's gone at this club now.' Nodding at Shearer, he said, 'We've bought him because we know, even with the great players we've got, this guy on my right's going to improve them.' All he had to do now was ask Les Ferdinand to surrender his number 9 shirt. Before they flew to Bangkok he took the player aside and told him about Shearer and his one request.* Surprised and perhaps not delighted to hear that a new centre-forward was on the way, Ferdinand nevertheless agreed. But by the end of the flight he was feeling less amenable, and some argy-bargy with the boss ensued. Eventually, he agreed to take the

---

* Shearer's single requirement was in fact soon followed by another: to be the team's penalty-taker. So Keegan then had to tell Peter Beardsley, the incumbent, to surrender penalty duties to the new man – a more serious concession than a mere shirt number. One wonders at what point resistance crumbled and 'request' actually became 'demand'.

number 10 shirt, which in turn put Lee Clark in a
sulk. Always a numbers game . . .

Whenever Keegan's managerial failings were under
debate the criticism that would recur was his cava-
lier indifference to tactics. He was still in thrall to the
Shankly mantra that football was 'a simple game complicated by coaches'. He believed that his job was to
let players play, without fear. It is a contradiction in
his strange character that on a business footing he was
the very opposite – not laissez-faire at all but a shrewd
deal-maker who knew his own worth and paid atten-
tion to the small print. Back in the days of negotiating his own transfers and striking his own bargains he
gave little quarter to the people on the other side of the
desk. By his own telling he played it cool and nearly
always got what he wanted. So why didn't he adapt
this hard-headed style to the high project of coaching?
If he had the nous to make a deal watertight, why not
a defence?

'Attack wins you games, defence wins you titles'
is a saying that never seemed to trouble Keegan.
Something changed his mind, however, for in October
1996 he sounded out Mark Lawrenson for a job as –
guess what? – defensive coach. The timing was odd,
because Newcastle were in the middle of a seven-match
winning run, including a memorable 5–0 thumping of

United.* No matter that Lawrenson, already employed as a pundit for the BBC, had no specific experience in defensive coaching, though by his account the most that was required of him was to 'observe'. As he told Ian Ridley in his Keegan biography, all seemed well on the training ground. The manager's rapport with the players was exceptional: 'He was always jolly, especially Friday mornings before a game. Get the ball out, make them feel fantastic because we need them tomorrow.'

Top of the league following the win against United, the team then fell into a slump, taking four points from the next 21. Whatever he might have projected in front of the players, Keegan was unhappy, only now it didn't concern just the results. Change was afoot behind the scenes. In common with other big clubs at this time the Newcastle board was preparing a flotation on the stock exchange. A new chief executive, Mark Corbridge, had been appointed to oversee the deal, and his burgeoning influence put Keegan's nose out of joint. The frenzy of business at St James's Park had diminished his status as manager, and he began to feel friendless. An initial handshake agreement with

* Crowned in the 83rd minute by Philippe Albert's exquisite chip over Schmeichel. How they would have loved to see just one of those goals go in the last time United had visited, in March.

chief executive Freddie Fletcher seemed to secure a compromise: Keegan would stay till the end of the season and then bow out. Results had picked up in the interim: a 7–1 tonking of Spurs, then 3–0 against Leeds. Maybe it would turn out for the best.

Only it didn't. On 7 January Keegan was summoned to an emergency meeting with the directors, led by Corbridge. Lawyers were also present. It later emerged that the club, anxious about the market, had demanded that he sign a two-year deal or else leave now. He was ready to go. It was agreed that he would collect the £1 million the board had offered him when the club was floated, which amounted to £600,000 after tax. Not bad as a leaving present, except that the flotation had raised £183 million. The Halls had made £110 million from a club that Kevin Keegan had rescued from the Third Division and transformed into a Premier League powerhouse in the space of four years.

'I don't think they gave me what I was worth,' he reflected. The story of the split occupies the first 20 pages of his 1997 autobiography, where he ties himself up in knots of contradiction. It wasn't about the money, he says, only the principle, except that it's also about the money. He doesn't want to look back, and yet he can't help looking back. He bears no animosity towards the club, only he's bitter as hell about the way they treated him. He reckoned that if he had taken a lawyer into the meeting, he would have nailed a proper compensation deal. But he wanted to leave with his head held high, without regrets. One out of two ain't bad.

St Teresa of Avila's famous line runs, 'More tears are shed over answered prayers than unanswered ones.' The prayers of the Newcastle faithful had been answered back in 1992, when Keegan made his second coming and then gave them nearly five years of delight and despair. Once news of his departure got out, imagine the monsoon of tears that fell over the Tyne. Better that he had gone and left them trophyless, or better if he had never come at all? She knew a thing or two about grieving, St Teresa.

Would Keegan have stayed had he won the league in 1996? It would certainly have given him leverage in the ensuing boardroom brouhaha. He would have been able not only to roar, Maximus-style, 'Are you not entertained?' but also 'Are you prepared to let go of a proven winner?' With only the first question satisfactorily answered the directors decided to take their chances. But Keegan might have had enough anyway. He didn't like being overshadowed, and he also might have wondered if he'd taken Newcastle as far as he could. Defending a league title is allegedly harder than winning it. Of course, it would have been nice to have had the choice.

He had made it clear that Newcastle was the only club he would ever manage. He probably meant it at the time. But once the dust had settled on their sundering he was ready for the next challenge. In fact, he wanted to reboot one of his old ventures, Kevin Keegan's Soccer Circus, a one-of-a-kind 'interactive football skills arcade'. No matter that so far it had met with bafflement and indifference, or that 'Soccer Circus' sounded like an American knock-off vaguely connected to football. It's unclear who made the initial approach to whom, but a meeting was arranged between Keegan and Mohamed Al-Fayed, the billionaire owner of Harrods and Fulham FC. If it wasn't quite a meeting of minds, it surely satisfied one man's hankering for celebrity and the other's for a patron with deep pockets.

Fayed listened to the proposals regarding the Soccer Circus, probably wondering like everyone else what the hell it was about, while being impressed by his man's enthusiasm and can-do. *His* proposal was for the ex-Newcastle manager to take over at his football club, in the role not of coach but of chief operating officer, to oversee the direction of the club and the appointment of a new manager. Fulham, still at their quaint Craven Cottage ground, had never won a major trophy and had last been in the top division 28 years ago. But Fayed was willing to spend big, and the personal incentive for Keegan was £750,000 a year with bonuses if he stayed at the club for three years. The aim was to become the 'Manchester United of the south'. The deal was done, and he had thrown in his lot with 'Mr Fayed'. Soccer Circus wasn't mentioned between them again.

The first casualty of the Fayed regime was manager Micky Adams, who had helped the club narrowly avoid non-league football and then got them promoted to the Second Division as runners-up the following season. Keegan, who may have seen a mirrored glint of his own rescue job at Newcastle, reckons he would have kept Adams had he started at Fulham earlier. Instead, he appointed his old mentor Arthur Cox as his assistant and got in his ex-England teammate Ray Wilkins as head coach. Fayed, impatient for success, gave Keegan carte blanche to modernise the club. This encompassed everything from the training ground to the renovation of the stadium to the new kit sponsorship by Adidas. Keegan's office was situated, somewhat eccentrically, at Harrods, perhaps a bit too close to the proprietor's, so operations were moved wholesale to

Craven Cottage.* On the pitch results were middling, the possibility of promotion always within reach. But as far as coaching went there were too many drivers in the car, both front- and back-seat. Wilkins and his assistant, Frank Sibley, took training, which was overseen by Arthur Cox, who reported back to Keegan, who reported to Fayed. Expectations would be less realistic in an owner who didn't know the game well. There may also have been an unacknowledged friction between the two ex-England pals. Keegan admired Wilkins, but they had never worked in management together, and their playing styles perhaps anticipated the difficulties that lay ahead. Keegan was all firecracker energy and forward thrust; Wilkins was more reflective, an artist who took his time and preferred the sideways pass. He was also less confrontational than Keegan, who on making a decision – e.g. to move a player on from the club – wanted it done straightaway. Wilkins was a dodger, and a procrastinator,

---

* Not all the changes were popular. A 'family' club, Fulham cherished its atmosphere of friendliness and tradition, best exemplified in the abiding presence of ex-Radio One DJ David 'Diddy' Hamilton as the Tannoy announcer. Years later, with Fulham in the Premier League, Diddy got the boot from the booth – the modernisers wanted fresh blood – causing an outcry. Once the *Sun* got involved with a 'Diddygate' campaign the club backtracked, and he was reinstated.

which to Keegan smacked of passivity. It would also have counted against Wilkins that his former loyalties in west London – QPR, Chelsea – made life at Craven Cottage tougher, whereas Keegan came with stardust on his shoulders and a proud northern pedigree.

Approaching the business end of the 1997–98 season Fulham were sitting pretty, until they lost their last three games, only qualifying for the play-offs on goal difference. When Fayed called Keegan into his office there was only one conversation on the agenda: he wanted Wilkins out and Keegan to take his place. In his autobiography Keegan sounds regretful that this had come to pass, and puts the decision on Fayed. But he was perhaps more complicit in the move than he let on. It wasn't just that his dynamism jarred with Wilkins's laid-back ways; he was probably itching to show that he could do a better job.* No immediate improvement was at hand, however; in the play-offs Fulham lost 2–1 on aggregate against Grimsby, and Keegan's big spenders were stuck for another season in the third tier.

But ambition never sleeps, or at least it never did when Keegan was around. His goal was to bring back the glory days of Fulham; if not the era of Johnny

---

* Wilkins later sued the club for £1 million.

Haynes, then surely the mid-1970s boom when George Best, Bobby Moore and Rodney Marsh wore the colours. If Chris Coleman's name doesn't carry quite the same éclat, he was nevertheless a record signing when he joined from Blackburn for £2.2 million, and he dropped down two divisions for the honour. The free-spending continued with Ian Selley from Arsenal, Paul Peschisolido from West Brom and a young defender, Steve Finnan, a future Champions League winner whom Keegan called one of his greatest all-time buys. Perhaps there was a touch of cronyism in him signing Paul Bracewell, Lee Clark and (aged thirty-seven) Peter Beardsley, plus a loan of Philippe Albert, as if trying to recreate the Newcastle spirit of '96. But they were good players, and he could afford them.

Fulham romped to the 1998–99 Second Division title with 101 points, 14 ahead of the nearest contender. Fayed dropped in to celebrate at Craven Cottage – by helicopter. On this, the final day of the season, black and white balloons were released before kick-off. Maybe it *was* Newcastle all over again. The fans were cock-a-hoop, though by the end of the game jeers could be heard amid the cheers as Keegan did his victory lap. For this was also his farewell to the club: he was off again, his head turned by the lure of a new job. *The* job, in fact. He had already been filling in there part-time since February. Much as he had loved the Fayed loot at Fulham, he found himself unable to resist the call of destiny.

9
THE BOSS

If Keegan regarded being captain of the national team as the greatest honour of his playing career, how would he have rated being manager? Let's imagine a CBE, a knighthood and an Order of the Garter rolled into one. St James's Park and Craven Cottage were all very well, but leading his team out as King of Wembley . . .

The job had come up after Glenn Hoddle, the incumbent since 1996, had aired in an interview with *The Times* his belief about karma and its operation on people with disabilities: 'You have to look at things that happened in your life and ask why.' Outrage poured down on Hoddle, who in a piquant illustration of his karmic musings was dismissed by the FA, though it's arguable that he was already heading for the door after a run of poor results and rumours of player discontent.

His fate highlighted the minefields of opprobrium that lay in wait for an England manager. Not that Keegan needed reminding: he had seen the job blow up in the faces of Alf Ramsey, Don Revie and prize 'turnip' Graham Taylor. But Hoddle was a fellow ex-international, one of his own generation, and if all it took to go wrong was an incautious remark, he would really have to be on his mettle. In front of a TV audience Keegan discussed how he would cope with the Impossible Job. One intense-looking young man put it to him, 'I think within eighteen months like every other England manager you'll be on the back page of the *Sun* as a vegetable.' Keegan replied that the press had already gone there: 'They asked me what vegetable I'd like to be.'

The FA had been short of options after Hoddle. The best managers in England at that time, Ferguson and Arsène Wenger, could not be prised away from club duties. If the FA couldn't find a candidate of proven achievement, they would have to settle for a character who would bring something else – passion, charisma, excitement – to the job. That narrowed it down to one name. Once Fayed granted his release from Fulham, they grabbed hold of Keegan like a shipwrecked sailor to a spar of driftwood. His initial agreement was to take charge of four games, his aim to help navigate the squad to the Euros in 2000. In his first press conference he invoked the example of 1966, a risky gambit for an England manager, but if anyone could whip up an optimistic mood, it was Keegan. And at least he wouldn't be including a faith healer in his entourage.

His appointment had an immediate effect. In a European qualifier against Poland, England revived their flagging campaign with a 3–1 win, and following a draw away to Hungary the call went up for him to take the job full-time. In May he did just that – and the results slumped. Their two June qualifiers against Sweden and Bulgaria were both drawn; a 6–0 walkover of Luxembourg and a 0–0 against Poland still left qualification on a wing and a prayer. Fortunately, a Swedish victory over Poland meant that England could qualify if they beat Scotland over two legs in November. At Hampden Park they won 2–0, and then, just to keep things in perspective, lost 1–0 at Wembley. It was an erratic and worrying run of form . . . but somehow they had crawled over the line. Keegan would be taking his team to the Euros.

His chapter on his England tenure – 'The Poisoned Chalice' – begins with a bald admission that no one but himself is to blame for what happened. 'I wasn't good enough,' he says. Yet with Keegan it's never quite straightforward, and far from taking sole responsibility he actually does quite a bit of fault-finding elsewhere. First of all, he breaks a lance against the FA. He was immediately put out when his plan to make Arthur Cox his assistant was rebuffed on the grounds that he was too old: they didn't want anyone over sixty. This decision came down from Howard Wilkinson (aged fifty-six), whose role as FA technical director might have raised eyebrows by itself.* Keegan recruited Cox on a part-time contract, and brooded, characteristically.

His mood was not improved when, at his first meeting, he asked about recruiting scouts to assess the opposition and keep tabs on his own players. Again, this request was brusquely turned down. The more he saw of the FA, the less encouraged he felt. As previous England managers had discovered, his employers tended to be pen-pushers, freeloaders and know-nothings, the sort of company blazers Ian Botham once described as 'gin-swilling old dodderers'. He was talking (in 1986) about the England Test selectors, but the breed was common to most sporting organisations. Could it have been such a revelation to Keegan? He must have heard enough from others to know what went on.

Let's accept that he'd not been an employee at Lancaster Gate before. But of his next perceived enemy

* Wilkinson changed his tune when the next England manager, Sven-Göran Eriksson, was permitted to bring in his own assistant, Tord Grip, aged sixty-two (and looked seventy-two).

he could claim no such innocence. His first press conference went well, the mood was upbeat, and Keegan had handled the questions with his usual mixture of sincerity and declamation. The media would have welcomed the new man – he gave good copy and at least presented a civil face, unlike dour old Glenn. Then, as he tells it, a sports photographer friend tipped him off about a couple of journos who were already gunning for him. Keegan reckoned it was because he didn't play favourites among the press (though he did play them elsewhere). Unlike, say, Terry Venables, he didn't cosy up to the football writers. He thought it beneath him. Even if that photographer was right, two hostile voices in the press were hardly going to derail his project. But Keegan, thin-skinned at the best of times, now discerned a whole conspiracy in the ranks, no longer two journalists bitching together but 'a movement against me from day one'.

Before his indignation burns a hole in the page he reverts to what he knows to be true. The results did for him, he admits, not the newspapers . . . So he was just having a moan. The actual reason he walked away is then revealed: he wasn't enjoying the job. That much became clear. In the icy altitudes of international competition Keegan's homespun, attack-minded football froze and died. Even before the tournament began, doubts haunted his squad selection, with six players over the age of thirty-two. And, remarkably, even *here* Keegan seeks an excuse: his players were either ageing and past their best or else too raw (Gerrard, Lampard, Gareth Barry) to make their mark. Was he so short-handed? He had Campbell and Adams in defence, Scholes and Beckham, Shearer and Owen – more than a decent spine. To those of us watching and waiting 'back home' (as the England song went in Mexico 1970) it still seemed possible we could get out of the group.

Our start was electrifying. In the first game against Portugal, in Eindhoven, England were 2–0 up after 20 minutes through Scholes and McManaman. Get in! Keegan looked fit to burst out of his Umbro shirt. But tremors of disquiet were perceptible in the face of Portugal's fluid movement and know-how. A couple of sighters had given the warning, and when Figo scored a worldie from 35 yards England were abruptly on the back foot. João Pinto equalised with a superb header, and with that wearying inevitability all England fans know Portugal took the lead in the second half and held on to it, as if by right. 3–2, and not even a hard-luck story. In Ian Ridley's Keegan biography, Tony Adams makes a point about the best way to defend, beginning with the front two. 'The team is a unit and everyone has to put a shift in,' he said. He conceded that Keegan set his teams up to be exciting and 'flamboyant', with lots of attacking options. 'Football for me is a balance and they didn't quite get the balance right.'

But optimism made another dissembling appearance in the next game, against Germany at Charleroi. I do recall whooping when Shearer's header got us in front, and we somehow sweated our way to a 1–0 win. It was a terrible game played by two hopeless sides, but hey, we'd beaten Germany! Shearer was both Keegan's talisman and his Achilles heel. The player had never reproduced his form of Euro 96 after a serious ankle injury, and yet Keegan made him the focal point of the team.* He ought to have had more faith in Owen, whom he inexplicably replaced with Heskey at half-time against Portugal. Romania were much the better side in our third game, and yet we were 2–1 up at half-time. Even at 2–2 we were going through to the quarters, until Phil Neville gave away a penalty in the 89th minute. 3–2, again. It was painful, but the Euros didn't suffer. England had not graced the scene.

'Everyone knows the way we play,' Keegan said afterwards. 'We like to get down the wings and get in crosses for our front men, and as long as I'm in

---

* Shearer announced his international retirement shortly after England's exit.

charge I hope we always will.' The predictability of this game plan ('Everyone knows . . .') ought to have worried him more. His reverence for the 'front men' was also telling; he couldn't see that different opponents might require a different approach. He had commented admiringly on the football played by Holland, Portugal and France – that is, by teams comfortable on the ball, strong in defence and quicksilver in attack. Martin Keown was one of the few players to be critical of his manager in public, calling him – in a phrase that will haunt Keegan to his grave – tactically naive. 'There's no point talking about tactics or formation if you can't even pass the ball,' Keegan said, which is true enough. But his England team was full of players who could pass the ball, if only they could be set up in a coherent shape.

It had been a demoralising campaign, and with the press up in arms Keegan might have been tempted to hand in his notice. That he didn't do so was perhaps down to the public goodwill he still had in his account (the win against Germany wasn't forgotten). But did he also feel this could be his last shot at the big time? As far as he was concerned, managing England was the pinnacle, the dream job. He had to make it work, not just to give the doubters one in the eye but to prove he was the winner he knew himself to be. He was *Kevin*

Keegan, for heaven's sake. Give him another chance and he could bend destiny to his will.

The problem, which took time to dawn on him, was that the dream job was nothing of the sort. Keegan thrived on the day-to-day routine of working with players, building a team spirit that was essentially the expression of his own personality. International football, set to a different rhythm, meant there were long periods with nothing to do. When he wasn't in there communicating with the players he felt no connection with the job. Another manager might have spent the in-between time working on strategies or scoping out the next opponents. But that wasn't Keegan's way.

Many have testified to his inspirational qualities as a manager. Steven Gerrard, a twenty-year-old when Keegan gave him his international debut, said, 'He made me feel like I was the best player in the world.' Instilling self-belief into a young person is a cherishable thing. But a team game demands more than individual self-belief; it needs discipline, a plan, awareness of one's part in the whole. The technical side didn't interest Keegan. The advice he had most enjoyed as a player was to 'go out there and drop some hand grenades'. Explosive players are great, and a joy to watch. Yet the ones who can do bomb disposal are just as important.

And so to a World Cup qualifier against Germany, Saturday 7 October 2000. The occasion was also a swansong to the old Wembley, which was about to be torn down and rebuilt. An omen right there. Keegan was already in a fragile mood after his mother had died the previous week. Bereavement and pressure made a horrible cocktail. His hopes of selecting Gerrard had been dashed when the player picked up an injury in training. This was doubly unfortunate, since the manager had spent the press conference talking him up. His late decision to play Gareth Southgate as a holding midfielder was leaked to the papers on the Friday, and all hell broke loose. Keegan was incandescent; he was being flayed before a ball had been kicked.

The skies were slate-grey at 3 p.m. In the 13th minute Scholes gave away a foul 35 yards out; while England dithered over forming a wall, Didi Hamann speared a low free-kick that skipped off the sodden turf and beat Seaman's flailing hand. It proved to be the winner in a dismal game, though the result was overshadowed by what happened next. As the fireworks went off to bid Wembley farewell, Keegan stumped through the rain to the tunnel, boos ringing in his ears. *When you walk through a storm* . . . His first port of call should have been the press conference, but instead he made for the dressing room, where he told the players he had

had enough and was off. Adams and Beckham tried to remonstrate with him, to no avail. Then David Davies, the FA's executive officer, turned up to take Keegan away for a private confab. But where? The corridor outside was rammed with reporters; the dressing room was thronged with players. The loos were the only option. 'The impending destruction could almost be smelled in the air,' recalled Davies, channelling Alan Partridge. In the toilet cubicle ('just about room for the two of us') Davies begged Keegan to reconsider, even appealed to his patriotism and loyalty to the players. He knew his man to be impulsive, and perhaps he could be talked round. But Keegan was unyielding, and even when the chief executive, Adam Crozier, came down to have a word he wouldn't budge.

Press to flush. Now wash your hands.

In an interview with Sky later that evening, Keegan sounded calm about his decision, as though he'd made it long ago. 'They've given me a fair run. There's nobody to blame but myself. Kevin Keegan has given it his best shot.' Again, the self-mythologising use of his own name struck a jarring note. His boss, Crozier, tried a diplomatic line, claiming that the decision to quit was 'a very courageous thing to do'. But was it really? Keegan said that hearing the boos from the Wembley crowd had helped him make up his mind – not very courageous at all, given that every England manager since Alf Ramsey had endured booing at one time or another. As for the press, Keegan might have deplored their sniping but it was as nothing compared to the vicious scorn heaped upon Bobby Robson and Graham Taylor.* When Crozier added that 'I think Kevin Keegan knew he was making the right decision for Kevin Keegan,' he inadvertently got closer to the truth.

One might call his time as England manager the chronicle of a dearth foretold. Dearth of ideas, of tactical acumen, of enthusiasm for the job. His win rate of 38.9 per cent is the lowest of any England manager. I think there's another reason why Keegan didn't succeed, and it's deeply connected to his personality: he wanted too much to be loved. The young Liverpool player who once said 'I like to be popular' hadn't changed. At heart he was puppyish. Martin Keown tells the story of being at the England base and going off to play snooker. On his way he encountered Keegan, who on hearing what was afoot said that he'd

---

* The young man in the TV audience who predicted that Keegan would end up being pilloried on the back pages like every other England manager got it spot on, time-wise: it took 18 months. But unlike Taylor, Keegan escaped being compared to a vegetable. Would a wet lettuce have been appropriate?

join him for a game. 'He was my boyhood hero,' says Keown, 'and here I was playing snooker with him.'

Stories also emerged of Keegan joining in card games when the squad was off-duty at the Euros, eager to be among the lads. While it says much of his conviviality, it also reveals a certain neediness. Good leaders grasp that sometimes you have to be alone, and aloof. You can't be a boss and a friend, unless you're David Brent. Shankly, Keegan's hero, understood that football management involved both the arm around the shoulder *and* the imperious glare. He was loved, but he also knew that he was feared. At Wembley that October night a less prickly character would have accepted the barracking, perhaps even drawn strength from it, and got on with the job. As someone who needed approval and the adulation of the crowd, Keegan would have found the occasion unendurable. The whistles and boos from the terraces would have lodged like arrows in his flesh. He had known the risks. So what was he doing there?

10
THE JOURNEYMAN

In February 2001 he turned fifty. His name was now spoken with a note of regret, of dashed hopes. He had become a member of a small and unenvied club of ex-England managers – and one of them he didn't speak to. His time as national coach had dissolved like a brief and unhappy dream. Rather like the screen idol who realises he has played his last major role, Kevin Keegan had to accept that he was no longer a star but a character actor. He would have to go back on the road again, in repertory.

Would anybody take a chance on him? He always brought drama, wherever he went, though not much in the way of dependability. His reputation carried a warning. Not for him the quiet exit; Keegan was one who flounced out, stormed off, baled, burned his boats. Gone Guy. It seemed that whenever he took a job his eye was always on the exits – and when he picked one it was often a surprise. His manner of leaving was definitive, like cancelling an account. When he quit a club he shed his interest in it – indeed, his interest in football. He admits that during his seven-year exile in Spain he rarely thought about the game. Is it idle to wonder how he occupied his time, other than by playing golf? He rarely makes reference to a film or a play or a TV show, and the only books he ever mentions are business manuals. If he has a hinterland, he has kept it well hidden.

Memories in football are short: a mere six months after his England debacle a club got in touch with Keegan, and a major club at that. Manchester City had spent the late 1990s frantically yo-yoing. From 1997–98 to 2001–02 they moved either up or down; five consecutive seasons ended in promotion or relegation. Joe Royle had overseen most of this chaotic hokey-cokey, including a spell in the Second Division, which they escaped by the skin of their teeth in a play-off final against Gillingham. The fans, long exposed to disappointment, probably took it in their philosophical stride when they were relegated from the Premier League in May 2001. Royle was out. Who could give the club a boost?

Keegan, ever the operator, had secured a five-year contract at Maine Road by the time he took his first press conference. He promised to 'turn around a sleeping giant' (don't you *wake* a sleeping giant?) and assured everyone he was up for the challenge. 'I enjoyed every minute of the England job,' he said, not very truthfully, 'but my skills are more suited to club management. I want to build something that people want to be part of.' The chairman, David Bernstein, was cock-a-hoop with his new appointment. He asserted that Keegan 'brings unique man-management and motivational qualities . . . And he'll bring something the club has lacked for twenty or thirty years – real style and flair.' Somewhere, perhaps, Malcolm Allison was smiling.

Keegan quickly identified his first task, which had nothing to do with football. A drinking culture had taken hold among the City squad, and like Eliot Ness in Chicago he was determined to clean the place up. He was also concerned by the seeming absence of dressing-room leaders. Never one to disdain the oldies-but-goodies, he signed Stuart Pearce from West Ham on a free. Pearce was thirty-nine. (I wonder if Peter Beardsley, forty, was also waiting by the phone after he heard of Keegan's appointment.) Significantly, Keegan brought in 'Psycho' not so much for his defensive capabilities, more as a bristling example of never-say-die commitment. This guy, he reminded his players, had once broken his leg during a game and tried to run it off. That was the mindset he was after. Crybabies were *out*.

Whatever Pearce brought to the table (the physio's) it was in fact Keegan's attacking players who made the difference in his first campaign. City finished champions of the First Division, ten points clear, with a goal tally of 108, the joint highest in their history. Shaun Goater was the first City player since Francis Lee in 1972 to score more than 30 goals in a season. Shaun Wright-Phillips – a protégé of Keegan's – Paulo Wanchope and Darren Huckerby contributed 40 league goals between them. Pulling the strings in midfield was Ali Benarbia, whom Keegan called 'the best signing of all my years in management'. Composed, almost visionary in his passing, Benarbia had won trophies with Monaco, Bordeaux and Paris Saint-Germain, and quickly became the fans' favourite. He was also a personable fellow, unlike the team's other midfield maestro, Eyal Berkovic, a spiky individualist whom Keegan never warmed to: 'If everything wasn't to his liking, he had a tendency to take it badly and throw a strop.' Could it be he reminded him of someone?

It became clear that City were operating at a higher level: they were a Premier League side in the wrong division. But if they were scoring for fun, they also had the worst defensive record in the top six; in September alone they conceded four goals in three separate games.

Keegan was delivering exactly as expected – goals galore from brilliant attacking formations, and who cared if they leaked a bit at the back. On the wings of this success he dipped into the transfer market so as to build muscle for their return to the Premier League. He splashed out on Nicolas Anelka and Sylvain Distin from PSG, and got Peter Schmeichel on a free from Villa. Following a poor start to the 2002–03 season, results picked up, including a 3–1 win over United in the last-ever derby at Maine Road. City finished ninth, which was decent enough but hardly answered to the vaulting ambition that had attended Keegan's arrival.

Any misgivings were put on hold while the club made its long-awaited transition to Eastlands and the new City of Manchester Stadium, which had previously hosted the 2002 Commonwealth Games. He was busy again in the transfer market. The good news was that he had offloaded Berkovic to Portsmouth. The bad news was that his star recruits, Robbie Fowler and Steve McManaman, had not had the galvanising effect anticipated, though they had massively inflated the wage bill. Keegan never struck gold as he had with Benarbia. Journeymen players came and went, sometimes without even making an appearance.

The club was not pushing on, and relations with the board began to fray. As usual, Keegan's main disgruntlement concerned money. Bernstein, the chairman, was a chartered accountant and handled the purse strings more cautiously than the manager liked. He almost sabotaged the Robbie Fowler transfer by belatedly contacting Leeds to tell them the deal was off unless he got a £500,000 reduction on the fee. Bernstein's view was that the club had spent big. Keegan's was that they had not spent enough. In the ensuing brouhaha about the club's direction it was the chairman who left.

In the meantime discipline had taken a nosedive. Keegan's limited pastoral talent had already been stretched by Richard Dunne's issues with alcohol, but after an interminable string of second chances the player had at last knuckled down. Having just shooed Berkovic out of the door Keegan had a brand-new problem player. At a club Christmas party twenty-one-year-old Joey Barton stoked the Yuletide spirit by putting out a cigar on the eyelid of a youth player – early notice of the brutish behaviour to come. Keegan had ambivalent feelings about Barton. On first seeing him as a teenage player flying into reckless tackles and making himself unpopular, Keegan's verdict was decided: 'a thug'. Yet after getting to know the player he discovered a thoughtful and articulate character beneath the feral boy from Huyton.* He would also have admired his competitiveness, a *sine qua non* of the Keegan ideal. Unfortunately, it came with a hair-trigger temperament that routinely saw him involved in brawls, arrests, court appearances.

'In the end, you just had to accept he got a kick out of hurting people,' Keegan reflected. It was hurting the club, too. One of Barton's earliest dismissals came on an evening in February 2004, during an FA Cup game at Tottenham. City were 3–0 down at half-time, and in the time it took to walk from the pitch to the dressing room Barton got himself sent off for swearing at the referee. (He had already given away the free-kick from which Ziege scored Spurs' third.) Keegan feared the worst, not just for the second half but for his job: City were on a streak of one win in 18 games. One wonders what he said to the players before they went back out, because he hasn't put it on record himself. Did he say anything, or has he forgotten? Barton's indiscipline

---

* It haunts me that Barton was raised in the same Liverpool neighbourhood where I grew up. We moved out in 1970, by which point Huyton's genteel village charm had long been buried beneath high-rise housing and low life expectations. It was a hard and depressed place, and I sometimes wonder how I might have coped with the hand Barton was dealt – I don't mean the demands and rewards of a Premier League footballer (I wish) but the character-forming terrors of a violent childhood.

might have cost his team. Instead, it became a night of legend, a Lazarus-like revival in which ten-man City somehow returned from the dead with four goals, the winner a Jon Macken header in stoppage time. The wildness of the contest was pure Keegan and maybe a small compensation for that painful 4–3 defeat at Anfield eight years earlier.

The euphoria was short-lived. City's hopes of a cup run ended in the next round, when United beat them 4–2. In the league they finished an underwhelming campaign 16th. Keegan was chafing at the financial restraints, believing the club needed to take risks in the transfer market. A familiar pattern of disaffection was by now in play. Once he realised the limitations of his squad he sought to buy new players, instead of trying to coach the ones he already had. The new chairman, John Wardle, may have been sympathetic but his pockets weren't deep enough to satisfy Keegan. When Anelka was sold the following season he was not replaced, and City lost some firepower. Whereas the club was happy with consolidation – a degree of security in the Premier League – Keegan saw only underachievement. There is also the sense of a child bored with his toys. He was easily distracted. Once the shine had gone from a project his magpie instinct was to look elsewhere.

This time there was no bang of the door, just a long, lugubrious whimper. He was unable to hide his disintegrating enthusiasm; by the end he was giving players two days off in the middle of the week because he preferred not to be there himself. He let the club know that he would not be extending his contract, which had one more season to run. Wardle, decent to a fault, suggested it might be better to bring forward his departure, and they negotiated a pay-off. No hard feelings. The 'sleeping giant', as described by Keegan, had been roused from its slumber, but as yet there were no giant strides. In the meantime its chief motivator had, not untypically, lost interest and checked out.

11
THE DUPE

You can't go back. In fact, he had already *gone* back, 15 years before, to manage Newcastle after gracing the club as a player. It had ended in tears and recriminations. To go back a second time was surely a mistake. But shrewder men than Kevin Keegan have succumbed to the siren call of vanity. Like the ageing rocker who goes on tour to promote his 27th album, Keegan looked in danger of becoming his own tribute act. But it was riskier than that. The fans who flock to see the ageing rocker are simply happy to know their hero can still play. Can still *stand*. The return of a manager to the Premier League is predicated on more than just affectionate remembrance: he has to prove himself all over again, and at an exactingly tough level. Keegan, now in his mid-fifties, had been out of the game for nearly three years. And the club he returned to was no longer the one he had loved.

While he had made many a smart deal in his career, he had also shown himself susceptible to foolishness. Andy McDaft, come on down. He tells a story in his

autobiography of how he and his fellow racing enthu-
siast Terry McDermott had once started up a gambling
syndicate, with high hopes of making a fortune. The
enterprise lost them thousands and they quickly abandoned it. In the hiatus following his departure from
City Keegan had another shot at reviving his Soccer
Circus, in which he had an almost altruistic belief –
a gift to 'the next generation of the leisure centre'.
He had put his own money into the project, and in
May 2007 gave an interview in the *Observer* to whip
up publicity. He sounded fed up with football, with
the enshrinement of money and its deadening effect
on competition. The idea of hauling a club from the
Championship to the Premier League, without a huge
financial outlay, was 'impossible' today. 'It doesn't
work like that. Not now.'

But Soccer Circus wasn't working either, and he had
to take on an investor to help shore it up. It was time to
start earning again. McDermott, Sancho Panza to his
Don Quixote, was the first to alert his old pal to the
possibility of coming back. Newcastle were in the dol-
drums again after Sam Allardyce's non-inspirational
tenure, and club owner Mike Ashley wanted a marquee
name to win over the fans. After failing to land Harry
Redknapp he settled on the idea of Keegan, whom he
addressed as 'King Kev'. But the power behind the

throne turned out to reside elsewhere. Keegan, flattered, felt the excitement of the chase, though at their
first meeting he didn't like the way Ashley tried to hire
him on the cheap (£1 million a year was his opening
offer). After conciliatory words at another meeting
Keegan negotiated his contract upwards to £3 million
a year, with compensation of £2 million if they got rid
of him.

All appeared set fair. Money had been promised
him, and he was assured the final say-so on every
player they signed. As to who would oversee the
transfers, that was moot. Ashley already had three of
his men installed: his business partner Paul Kemsley;
Tony Jimenez, a property developer with links to the
South American market; and a casino owner named
Derek Llambias, now managing director. This was the
core of Ashley's 'cockney mafia', whose experience in
football management was almost nil. If that cronyism
didn't bother him, Keegan would surely have heard
the alarm bells when another insider, Dennis Wise,
was hired as director of football, in charge of scouting
players in Europe. The last time he had seen Wise was
as an unused sub on his England bench. How had he
wangled such a flash job for himself?

More pressing than the backroom shenanigans
was the team's dire league run, without a win since

mid-December. It had included a 5–1 spanking by Man Utd at St James's Park. Newcastle were grazing the relegation zone by the time Keegan enjoyed his first victory after nine games, 2–0 at home to Fulham. That was followed by a 4–1 thrashing of Spurs at White Hart Lane.* They got through April undefeated, before closing the season with losses to Chelsea and Everton. His spell so far had run hot and cold, with no reliable indication of where the club was heading or whose hand was on the tiller.

Interviewed after the Chelsea game Keegan was in disillusioned mood. He knew how far off the pace his team was: 'This league is in danger of becoming one of the most boring but great leagues in the world,' he said. 'The top four next year will be the same as the top four this year.' He conceded that if the owners were to back him, Newcastle could finish fifth, top of the other mini-league. But he saw no chance of breaking into the elite. His relationship with Ashley was fine: 'I get on great with the owner because I never talk to him.' It was not just the club's failure to dent the top four that bothered him. His own diminished status

---

* A game which I happened to attend. I noted in my diary, 30 March 2008: 'I couldn't help enjoying it, and feel pleased for Kev, hopping about on the touchline. Could this be the start of something for him, or is it merely the crest of a slump?'

was palpable. Alex Ferguson, on his perch, had left him for dust as a rival. Privately, he was also fuming about the club's botched attempt to sign Luka Modrić from Dinamo Zagreb, laying the blame squarely on Jimenez, who said the player was 'too lightweight for English football'. With experts like that . . .

Judging by the way Keegan recounts the saga in his autobiography, he had walked into a nest of vipers. He was given to understand that talking directly to Ashley was discouraged, if not actually *verboten*. This came from Jimenez, who seemed to have appointed himself consigliere to the capo. He insisted that in future any club business should be conducted through him. This was management of a kind Keegan hadn't dealt with before. His misgivings began to multiply. Advised to check out a Saint-Étienne striker, Bafétimbi Gomis, Keegan duly took a flight to France to watch him play in a Ligue 1 game. On the evidence of 90 minutes he could tell that Gomis wasn't up to snuff, a verdict that Dennis Wise – seated three rows behind – seconded. Job done.

Days passed before Keegan got a late-night phone call from Llambias, with the news that they had put in an offer of ten million euros . . . for Gomis. Unable to believe what he was hearing, he phoned the club secretary the next morning for an explanation. Yes, they had made an offer for the player, and it had been rejected. It hardly mattered. Keegan had just been served notice that transfers were not under his control. Nor would he be involved in contract talks with players already at the club. One can sympathise with his grievance – up to a point. The problem was that his own transfer targets were so unrealistic as to look faintly barmy. Luring Thierry Henry from Barcelona? David Beckham from LA Galaxy? Frank Lampard from Chelsea? Well, a man's reach should exceed his grasp, but anyone could see such a wish list was delusional. Only imagine the mutual incomprehension that reigned in the Newcastle boardroom, at least when they bothered to use it. If they deigned to talk to one another, it was mostly on the phone.

It dawned on Keegan, eventually, that he had been naive. Ashley had called him 'the most honest man in football', but on his tongue the words sounded like a slur. Matters came to a head early in the 2008–09 season, when the club openly bypassed Keegan to sign two players. The transfer policy at St James's Park already had the air of a bingo night. Jimenez would reel off lists of players' names, who were then discarded or forgotten. Other players were being offered or sold to whittle down the wage bill. By August the club had brought in Danny Guthrie from Liverpool, Sébastien Bassong (a future Newcastle player of the year) and the Argentine winger Jonás Gutiérrez, who was known for pulling on a Spider-Man mask to celebrate his goals.

Keegan was in need of a superhero. Instead came a bombshell that Wise and Jimenez were bringing in a striker named Xisco from Deportivo La Coruña (for £5.7 million) and a Uruguayan midfielder, Ignacio González, from Valencia. He hadn't heard of either of them. He phoned Wise to seek clarification; Wise told him that González was a top prospect, and he could check clips of him on YouTube. Super scouting! Having gone online Keegan was no more enlightened as to why Newcastle might want or need such a player. This was disconcerting. It was also belittling: the deals had been done behind his back, and the players were already in the country. So much for the guarantee that his would be the final word on transfers. A message reached him that Ashley wanted to meet, face to face. He must have hoped his relationship with Keegan could be yanked from the fire. A confidential pow-wow was set up at an address in London – so confidential that Keegan spotted the Sky cameras waiting outside. It was the club's ploy to have pictures of the manager arriving and thus show the fans that they meant to conciliate him. Without further ado Keegan gave the place a bodyswerve.

The dream was over. He made his resignation announcement shortly afterwards, explaining that his position had become untenable. He could not manage at a club where he had no executive powers. He apologised to the fans, declaring they deserved better. (Little did they know that their misery was just beginning.) With that done, he entered the long, complicated process of filing a claim against Ashley for constructive dismissal. Newcastle counter-sued for £2 million, claiming Keegan had breached his contract. His second spell as manager had lasted eight months.

What are we to make of this misadventure? On the one hand, Keegan presents a plausible case that he was duped, set up as front-of-house while Ashley's clown courtiers parcelled out the power between them. On the other, he ought to have been more circumspect about taking the job in the first place. He had been in football long enough to be able to spot a charlatan, and some research into the backgrounds of Jimenez, Llambias et al. could have saved him a great deal of trouble. As for Ashley, Keegan was repelled by his yobbish, pint-with-the-fans persona, but he also had a weakness for rich men and was all too willing to be seduced. One more chance to be the saviour of St James's Park.

It might be argued, however, that the return of King Kev was doomed anyway, even without Ashley and his goons' rodeo. For by 2008 Keegan was a man out of time. Football chairmen were proverbial as hard-nosed types, but now they came with a retinue of backers and consultants who had their own ideas about a club's financial structure. The role of manager was located somewhere at the base of the pyramid. Keegan was slow to twig this. Perhaps he had imagined himself pinning on his sheriff's star and running things again in Dodge, just like the old days. But Dodge had changed, radically, and as a Wild West hero he looked old-fashioned, toting a six-gun while the rest were carrying bazookas. The goodwill of the fans was there, but did anyone listen to the fans any more?

12
THE GHOST

The original meaning of the word 'disappoint' is to dispossess or deprive, literally to 'undo the appointment of'. Which sounds a lot like being given the boot. As a manager Kevin Keegan was never sacked; he quit every job on his own terms. But he was certainly *disappointed* in the sense we use the word now. Having left Newcastle for a second time he would have felt let down, and possibly something worse. He had been traduced by Ashley and his minions, given a lesson in the unscrupulous methods of the modern football hierarchy. Anyone would feel aggrieved.

I wonder how Keegan coped with the hurt of being discarded in the days and weeks following his departure. He must have suspected that his time in football was up. Wherever the fault lay in the wreckage of NUFC, there would be few clubs, if any, eager to call on his services. He had lived happily outside football before, for years, but there had always lingered the possibility of being tempted back in. The return of the exile. Keegan is one of those male stars, like Mick

Jagger or Martin Amis, who remain in our mind's eye full of youthful swagger, all tightened and tuned for maximum efficiency. And with a beauty in them that goes beyond explanation, as beauty always will. But unless you die young, age will exert its slow gravitational pull, and you end up past your prime, shunted into the sidings, no longer relevant. As Ian Hunter's peerless lament has it:

> And you gotta stay young, man,
> You can never be old . . .*

It's coming to all of us, sooner or later. Maybe the trick is in the timing, to get out of the business before every other face around you is a young person's. Keegan had spent most of his professional life being noticed, and listened to, and adored. A continuous cavalcade of admirers, all watching you. No ego could resist it. But he must have known there would come a moment when the parade had gone by, and he was left on his own. All those empty days ahead. Driven characters, even after a lifetime of achievement, will wonder if they could have done more with their talent.

---

* 'All the Way from Memphis' (1973), Mott the Hoople, written by Ian Hunter. © Universal Music Publishing Group.

(They don't stop being driven.) Success had once been his true companion. But whoever said that success was there to stay?

In my end is my beginning.[*] Keegan published his first autobiography in 1977, at the age of twenty-six, just as he was about to leave Anfield for Hamburg. He was probably the most famous footballer in Europe at the time, and about to become the richest. So we might have expected his mood to be expansive, maybe a little nostalgic as he reflected on his golden years. *Au contraire*. In the book's opening chapter he sounds defensive about his move abroad and narked by those who accuse him of ingratitude. He owes Liverpool nothing, he says, because he has already given them everything in terms of commitment. Yes, the club had made him a star, but a great club isn't necessarily a perfect one. He harped on his disappointment with the way LFC handled Shankly, its petty treatment of him after he left. He especially resented a demeaning episode when the club travelled to Bruges for the second leg of the 1976 UEFA Cup final. They invited Shankly to join them, but then ruined the gesture by putting him in a different hotel from the squad.

[*] T. S. Eliot, 'East Coker', *Four Quartets* (1944).

And that's just for starters. He recalls arriving at Liverpool and meeting another young hopeful, John McLaughlin, whom the other players rated highly ('They are the ones who really know'). Keegan soon understood why. McLaughlin was a cool-headed midfielder, unhurried on the ball and clever with a pass. Then Shankly dropped him, and he became a marginal player. After a few years a knee injury did for him. When Keegan next encountered him he was twenty-five and on the dole in Liverpool. A hard-luck tale that could have happened to any player. But Keegan had other stories that didn't reflect well on his former employers. His closest friend at LFC, Peter Cormack, was a brilliant Scots playmaker who also suffered an injury and lost his place. The club was not supportive of him, according to Keegan, and he moved on. They also behaved shabbily with Alec Lindsay, and unpardonably towards Chris Lawler, both times about money. That he was aggrieved on his teammates' behalf speaks well of him, though it also put potential suitors on notice: *Don't mess with me.*

That combative attitude shaped him. To watch him perform you sense the will of a player furiously pushing himself, damned if he's not going to give 100 per cent, or 1,000 per cent, or whatever the current rate of total commitment stands at. Of his fitness to lace

Best's boots we have heard, nor could he rival those languid flair players of the 1970s – Tony Currie, Alan Hudson, Stan Bowles. But he wasn't *that* far behind as an entertainer, and none of those players gave themselves to the cause like he did. Keegan didn't carry Liverpool to their 1970s zenith single-handedly. But I think it can plausibly be claimed that the club would not have won half so much without him. He was a team player not just in the sense that he 'gave his all'; I mean that his work rate and his involvement made his teammates up their game. He made those around him better.

It was this ability to inspire that determined the second act of his career. That, and the example of Bill Shankly. The young shaver who arrived from Scunthorpe could not have anticipated the profound force of personality his manager wielded. 'Manager' hardly covers it. Shankly was his champion, his press agent, his guru and maybe his surrogate father. I don't think it's outlandish to describe what they had as a love affair – chaste, of course, but intense, and lasting. No wonder Keegan, open-hearted and needy, saw the possibility of emulating Shanks. He had been the inspiration of teams as a player; why not again, from the dugout? It was an easy decision to make. Easy – and wrong. Shankly's character, already formidable, was sharpened by his time as a hard-bitten sergeant in the RAF, dealing with young men in wartime.

Keegan could match him for sentimentality, but not for his steeliness or his ruthlessness. Nor did he have around him the canny old heads of the Boot Room, to report, to advise, to mediate. Even with his loyal retainer McDermott at his side, King Kev ruled alone, a one-man band. Sometimes you can want something too badly. You choose not the thing you're good at, but the thing you'd like to be good at. Isn't it obvious by now where Keegan's true calling lay? In the final chapter of his latest (and last?) autobiography he is guilty of a flagrant untruth: 'I feel privileged to have made a life from the sport I would have played for nothing.' *Sorry?* Kevin Keegan, as this book has probably made clear, is a man who regards money and the making of it as a cornerstone of his life. I don't blame him for that. But it's far too late to present himself as someone who'd have played for free. As a twenty-something millionaire he would have curled his lip at a footballer who said such a thing.

Off the field Keegan excelled in two regards. One was motivational genius, instilling confidence into his players and persuading them of their own value. The other was a near-mercantile aptitude for a smart deal. In an era just on the cusp of player power Keegan left the rest of the field standing. Money was the one subject on which he always kept his head. Even as a twenty-year-old he had impressed Bill Shankly on first meeting with his negotiation of an extra five quid a week. Combine those skills and you may discern the lost second act of his career. Kevin Keegan ought to have been the greatest agent of them all. Imagine him showing up to make the deal public. He already had the car and the aviator shades; put him in a decent suit and watch him swagger through the press, the snappers and the gawkers. Likely as not the shortest man in the room, he could depend on his personality and charisma to bewitch all-comers. Imagine him sitting down with the chairman and directors and explaining exactly what he and his client wanted. He would have been irresistible.

The problem with agenting is that it's work done behind the scenes. There is lucre, but no lustre. As an outward-facing personality Keegan needed to feel the love, and no one really loves an agent, apart from their clients. He was a romantic and a cheerleader for entertainment. So he donned his Umbro tracksuit like a knight of old would his armour. He chose the way of the training ground and the scouting trips and the press conferences. Perhaps he enjoyed some of it. But with these duties came the ancient art of knowing how to beat an opponent, not just through the intricate detail of tactics and formations but through those famous mind games that he never learned to master. 'A cauldron of seething excitations': that is Freud's description of the id, the mind's unstable complex of urges and drives. It's an even better description of Kevin Keegan. His emotions were so close to the surface you could almost read them on his skin. He was always at their mercy, helplessly sincere and vulnerable, but also prickly and impetuous. In a battle of wits Keegan was an unarmed combatant. If he felt he was losing the fight, his default response was to walk.

Considered as a whole, his career looks lopsided. World-class player, economy-class manager. But to view Keegan's career as unfulfilled is simply mistaken. From the time he played for Liverpool and won a cabinetful of silverware he was immunised against failure for the rest of his life. Everything that came after is insignificant next to the period from 1971 to 1980. You cannot judge the value of achievement in chronological terms. He had staked everything on becoming a great player, and he had won. All we may add is that he was *less great* as a manager, and even then he showed a kind of greatness in his daring.

If we feel a sense of disappointment, that is inevitable. Ninety-five per cent of being a fan is disappointment.

Most clubs lose, most managers fail, but you go on being a fan. The only failure to be feared is failure of the imagination, which is where stupidity and prejudice and hatefulness are born. (It starts with tragedy chanting and escalates from there.) But failure in football, in sport, that's what reveals character. If you don't know how to lose, you don't know how to live. As Beckett said, 'Try again. Fail again. Fail better.'*

Where is he now? In football you're a long time retired, and unless you take a job on TV or radio your name slips out of public consciousness. Only think of the vast mute armies of ex-footballers out there, playing golf, mooching around the garden, tending all those memories of games gone by. Some of them were famous once. For a while in the 1970s Keegan was the most famous of them all. I find it hard not to think of him as an unquiet ghost, still tuned to the sound and fury of the crowd. *Oh, my Keegan and my Toshack long ago!* When I watch clips of him playing on YouTube I wonder how he has come to terms with his own legend. That darting, quicksilver figure, stocky yet agile, haunts my mind's eye. His LFC shirt glows like the red of a London Routemaster,

* Samuel Beckett, 'Worstward Ho' (1983).

sometimes crimson, sometimes scarlet depending on the film stock. I thrilled to that sight. I still do.

But actually, what is he up to? A search on Google brings up an advert for CSA Celebrity Speakers, where he numbers among the hirelings for business events and motivational talks. On their website, a review of his performance at a recent gig: 'Kevin Keegan had a great balance between humour and seriousness; with personalised and informative content. He had good contact with the audience and was inspirational.' Thus writes a Bespoke Events Organiser, somehow contriving to make him sound pretty ordinary. He's also featured on After Dinner Speakers & Comedians, his price listed as £5,000–10,000 (the same as Baroness Mone further down the page). The reviews are glowing, like this from the Football Safety Officers Association: 'Kevin Keegan was the best we have ever had our members have all said the same. A quote from the FSOA would be. How do you follow that? We would recommend Kevin to anyone and would at some point ask him to return for us.'

I like the slightly cautious 'at some point'.

Once in a while you may hear the moaning of the ghost. For those who barely notice football his sudden manifestation in the news headlines must have been doubly shocking – first on account of what he said, second because his name had fallen into obsolescence. *Kevin Keegan – is he still going?* On 4 October 2023 *The Times* carried a story about a public event in Bristol where Keegan, a guest speaker, said that he was unimpressed by female pundits. Or, in his words, 'I don't like to listen to ladies talking about the England men's team at the match because I don't think it's the same experience. I have a problem with that.' The comment drew some applause, and he continued, 'The presenters we have now, some of the girls are so good, they are better than the guys. It's a great time for the ladies. But if I see an England lady footballer saying about England against Scotland at Wembley and she's saying, "If I would have been in that position I would have done this," I don't think it's quite the same. I don't think it crosses over that much.'

The garbled grammar has a touch of the saloon bar about it – a saloon bar at some point in the 1970s. He's not an unregenerate chauvinist. He rates some female presenters more highly than men. But what betrays him is the language. (It betrays us all in the end.) The phrases 'England lady footballer' and 'It's a great time for the ladies' would make you giggle if he wasn't being serious. You suspect that he believes 'lady' is a rather gallant way of referring to women, whereas it simply shows how old he is, and how outdated his thinking. I wonder if Jean ever thought of telling him, 'Don't say "ladies" – it makes you sound like a twit.' Maybe she thought it was too late to re-educate him. In an interview with the *Guardian* in 2011 Keegan said that Jean takes football 'with a pinch of salt'. But she's sensitive, too: 'After matches, if you've lost she knows not to say too much for about 24 hours while you get over it, and if you've won she knows I might take her out at night.'

Very handsome of him!

There was an outcry on social media. When is there not? Poor Kev had embarrassed himself, and Lianne Sanderson, ex-Lioness, spoke for many when she posted, 'I would absolutely "Love it" if he would shut up!' The ironies kept coming when Keegan acclaimed the late Brian Moore as the best TV commentator. Now Moore *was* brilliant, and by all accounts a true gent, but he and Keegan did share one of the great terrible exchanges in commentating history. Ripple-dissolve to the 1998 World Cup in France, as England fronted up to Argentina in a penalty shoot-out. As David Batty prepared to take his spot-kick, Moore asked Keegan if he thought Batty would score. 'Yes,' said Keegan. Batty missed, and England were out. Difficult to decide who's more at fault, Moore for asking the question or Keegan for answering it. Call it a draw.

The 'lady footballer' remarks were mulled and mocked and quickly forgotten. The public moved on in search of fresh outrage. Did the fuss even bother Keegan? I didn't notice any follow-up defence from him, any claims that he was misquoted. Nor was there a boilerplate apology in the sorry-if-anyone-was-offended style (i.e. not really sorry at all). Maybe he is fine about speaking his mind, and if 'the ladies' don't like it, well . . .

The longer the distance from a sporting hero's glory days, the more melancholy become our reflections. Because it's not just them we lament, it's the memory of our own investment – of our innocent delight – in their achievements. I think one of the things I miss most about Keegan is his spontaneity, that sense of not quite knowing what he would do next. Football feels starved of such characters at the moment. Whatever else can be said about him, he was his own man, cussed and unbiddable. I seem to be already talking about him in the past. This might be a way of saying goodbye to the player I loved. Or goodbye to the boy who saw him in his prime and cried when he left Liverpool.

ACKNOWLEDGEMENTS

Thanks to my editor at Faber, Angus Cargill, and to Anne Owen, Hannah Turner, Sophie Clarke and Kishan Rajani. Also to Jon Wood, Safae El-Ouahabi, Ian Bahrami and, as ever, to Rachel Cooke.

Plus a huge roar from the sofa for *Shoot!* magazine, which started me off.

BIBLIOGRAPHY

Keegan, Kevin, *Kevin Keegan* (1977)
Keegan, Kevin, *Kevin Keegan: My Autobiography*
  (1997)
Keegan, Kevin, with Daniel Taylor, *Kevin Keegan:
  My Life in Football* (2018)
Ridley, Ian, *Kevin Keegan* (2008)

Bracewell, Michael, *England Is Mine* (1997)
Gerrard, Steven, *Gerrard: My Autobiography* (2006)
Glanville, Brian, *The Story of the World Cup* (1997
  edition)
Hamilton, Duncan, *Answered Prayers* (2023)
Lewis, Ted, *Jack's Return Home* (1970)
Niven, Alex, *The North Will Rise Again* (2023)
Shankly, Bill, *Shankly* (1976)
Thompson, Phil, *Stand Up Pinocchio* (2005)

Thanks to: thetimes.com, theguardian.com,
youtube.com, lfchistory.net, thisisanfield.com, liver-
poolfc.com, liverpoolecho.co.uk, theanfieldwrap.com

PHOTO CREDITS